Living LANGUAGE

LANGUAGE AND STYLE

Michael Jago

Hodder & Stoughton

A MEMBER OF THE HODDER HEADLINE GROUP

Acknowledgements

Copyright Text:

The publishers would like to thank the following for their kind permission to reproduce copyright material:

Recipe for Cornish Pasty Pie reproduced from *Complete Cookery Course* by Delia Smith with permission of BBC Worldwide Limited, © Delia Smith (1992); William Hague's speech, 10 October 1997, reproduced with permission of Conservative Central Office, Westminster; extracts from *Diana* by Andrew Morton, reproduced with permission of Michael O'Mara Books Ltd; 'Coney in Sight' by F.J. Taylor, reproduced with permission of *Shooting Times and Country Magazine*, first appeared in *Shooting Times and Country Magazine*, 22–28 July 1998; 'The Woman Who Hangs Today' by William Connor, © The Mirror Group, first appeared in the *Daily Mirror*, 13 July 1955; 'The Boy William Did Well' by Matthew Parris, © News International Ltd, first appeared in the *Sun*, 26 June 1997.

Every effort has been made to trace copyright holders of material reproduced in this book. Any rights not acknowledged will be acknowledged in subsequent printings if notice is given to the publisher.

Orders: please contact Bookpoint Ltd, 39 Milton Park, Abingdon, Oxon OX14 4TD. Telephone: (44) 01235 400414, Fax: (44) 01235 400454. Lines are open from 9.00 – 6.00, Monday to Saturday, wtih a 24 hour message answering service. Email address: orders@bookpoint.co.uk

British Library Cataloguing in Publication Data
A catalogue record for this title is available from The British Library

ISBN 0 340 73082 X

First published 1999
Impression number   10 9 8 7 6 5 4 3 2 1
Year   2005 2004 2003 2002 2001 2000 1999

Copyright © 1999 Michael Jago

Cover photo from The Ronald Grant Archive
Typeset by Fakenham Photosetting Limited, Fakenham, Norfolk NR21 8NL
Printed in Great Britain for Hodder & Stoughton Educational, a division of Hodder Headline Plc, 338 Euston Road, London NW1 3BH by Scotprint Ltd, Musselburgh, Scotland

Contents

'My special thanks to my son James without whose computer expertise and sacrifice of so much summer holiday this book would never have been written.'

Preface

This book aims to help students develop at their own pace the skills necessary for a critical and enlightening reading of non-literary texts in English. It has been written to meet the needs of those preparing for any one of a number of Advanced Level, GNVQ, or similar examinations that require the ability to analyse various types of written material. Such students, whether first-time or adult returners, whether learning through traditional classes, through Open Learning or by private study, should find help and reassurance here.

At a general level many syllabuses aim to develop the students' analytical skills in their response to, description and explanation of, and comment upon, a variety of English texts. This book aims to help the student acquire the techniques for doing this in a systematic and effective way. No previous knowledge of language study is assumed, as each chapter provides sufficient information and theory for the examination of the data under discussion. Although such a relatively short book cannot hope to include every possible type of text, it does attempt to give sufficient theory and practice so that the student can tackle more demanding texts with confidence.

A note on the types of text included. Many good reasons exist for not making the traditional division between literary and non-literary texts. Certainly, a range of critical techniques can be applied successfully to either. However, numbers of students are now involved in a wide range of courses that necessitate the study of language other than in a literary context, and for many of them literary texts can often appear difficult or even irrelevant. This book is designed particularly to help them, but it should prove equally valuable to those students already familiar with the linguistic criticism of literary texts.

Each chapter introduces a topic by sample texts, analysed and commented upon, followed by a variety of suggested activities. Though the chapters are ordered deliberately, there is considerable cross-referencing and re-examination of textual examples, so that individual chapters can be used with profit. The chosen texts and associated activities vary in length and difficulty, allowing both beginners and more advanced students to make progress. Each chapter concludes with some recommended further reading, while the final chapter takes a look at how to improve the examination answer script itself.

1 Tiny Texts

In this first chapter you will take a look at a variety of texts. You will begin learning techniques of enquiry into language. The aim is to explain why you respond to texts in the way that you do. You will discover how to find the evidence for your responses. You will learn methods of 'pulling texts apart' that reveal the ways in which those texts were originally put together by their writers.

What is a text?

Throughout this book you will be examining many examples of both spoken and written language used in a variety of ways. Such examples are normally called 'texts'. All subjects need a set of technical terms so that you can understand and discuss them, and the study of language is no exception. A text can be defined quite simply as 'any stretch of spoken or written language'. This may seem a little vague, but at this stage it is more important to examine some examples than to worry about more precise definitions.

A clue to the nature of texts is contained in the word itself. Both 'text' and 'textile' mean essentially the same thing: something that is woven together. A textile is made by interlacing separate strands of material into a whole. The material may be wool, cotton or silk; thick, thin or very fine; it may contain any number of colours or patterns. These elements may be combined in endless ways to produce a material suitable for a particular purpose and type of person, whether it's yellow silk pyjamas for a millionaire or a chequered shirt for a lumberjack.

Likewise, any text is woven together with words. The words may be unusual or commonplace, old-fashioned or modern slang, fiendishly difficult or childishly simple. What's more they may be combined into various sentence patterns: long and complex, short and simple, or some mixture of the two. The possibilities are infinite. And it is this infinite variety that allows the creation of new and exciting texts.

Keeping this concept of variety in mind you are now ready to examine a random selection of short texts in order to discover just what makes each different from the others. For reasons of space some parts have been omitted in order to shorten some of the texts, but this will not affect your evaluation. To help you with this initial exercise, here are some questions you should find answers for:

1 What is the text about?
2 Why was the text written?

3 Who specifically did the writer intend should read the text?

4 In what way is the use of language different in each text?

ACTIVITY 1

At least 90 minutes should be allowed for this first exercise. If less time is available, then the number of texts surveyed should be reduced. However, fewer than six is unlikely to be very productive.

1 In small groups read and discuss the following nine texts. Nominate one person in each group to write down your agreed answers to the above four questions for each text. If you disagree then record the alternative answers for discussion.

2 Now discuss the areas of disagreement. You may not be able to resolve these but you should understand why differences of opinion have arisen. It is likely, for instance, that you may disagree with the answer to question 2 on some of the texts. There could, of course, be several reasons for writing a text!

3 Finally, compare your answers to question 4 for each text. Have you noticed at least one way in which each text uses language individually?

TEXT 1

THURSDAY

A Stylish mix of current trax and club classics.

Half Price

admission all night (with ID) for 999 services

2 Drinks for the price of one

B4 midnight

£2 B4 10.30 £4 after
**Over 19s. Smart casual dress
No T-shirts, No trainers.**
Valid @ management's discretion. R.O.A.R.

TEXT 2

Visa Card Payment Protection – wise up to the benefits

Please don't think that we're trying to put the frighteners on you but we would like you to protect yourself against the unpleasant side of life. Accidents, illness and redundancy, for instance. If any of those should put you out of work the last thing you want to be worrying about is paying your credit card bill each month.

That's why we recommend that all of our customers arrange Payment Protection. For just 67p per £100 of your outstanding balance, you can be reassured that 5% of your outstanding balance will be paid each month if you cannot work due to an accident, injury or involuntary unemployment. The entire balance will be paid in the event of death.

The small premium is added to your bill each month. And if your balance is zero, so is your premium.

Surely this is one offer of protection you can't refuse.

TEXT 3

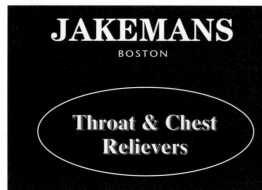

JAKEMANS

BOSTON

Throat & Chest Relievers

Jakemans famous original Throat & Chest Relievers are made with only the finest ingredients, carefully blended to obtain an effective medicated sweet with a unique mouthwatering flavour.

Not only are they effective for chesty coughs and sore throats, many people who suffer from asthma, bronchitis and catarrh tell us they get most effective relief from them.

People buy them just for their mouth watering and refreshing taste.

ONCE TASTED THEY WILL BE YOUR FAVOURITE MEDICATED SWEET.

TEXT 4

WARNING
THESE PREMISES ARE PROTECTED BY NU-CAM C.C.T.V.
24 HR VIDEO SURVEILLANCE IN OPERATION
TEL: NU-CAM SYSTEMS
FREEPHONE 0800 7315607

TEXT 5

ARE YOU A GOOD LISTENER?

Do you:

- Always try to give people your undivided attention?

- Let them sit in silence and collect their thoughts if they need to?

- Question them gently, tactfully and without intruding?

- Encourage them to tell their story in their own words and in their own time?

- Refrain from offering advice until you've heard what their problem is?

- Always try and see their point of view even though you may not agree with it?

Or do you:

- Look around the room or glance at your watch while they're talking?

- Finish their sentences for them, and correct their grammar?

- Butt in to tell them how you once had a similar problem

- Make a snap judgement based on their accent, dress or personal appearance?

- Tell them what you would do in their position?

- Say you understand before you've heard what their problem is?

The Samaritans

TEXT 6

feel free
Liberate yourself from punishing slimming regimes and avoid that built-in failure factor. At last success can be yours at Slimming World, where it isn't a sin to eat and enjoy life!
Slimming WORLD
WE'RE WITH YOU ALL THE WAY

TEXT 7

THE CAR-BUYER'S GUIDE

During 1996 over 500,000 cars were stolen in England and Wales. 30% of all stolen cars are not recovered - many are disguised by the thief and sold to innocent purchasers.

This "Guide" aims to prevent you from buying a stolen car. Please use our advice to protect yourself.

Research

△ Decide what make and model you are interested in.
△ Find out where the vehicle's identification numbers should be.
△ Consider taking an independent qualified examiner with you.

Private Advertisements

△ Can you **identify** the vendor? Beware of mobile telephone numbers (which may not be traceable).
△ Beware of "between 5pm and 6pm" type adverts. Is this a phone box? Try calling outside the specified hours.
△ Does the vendor hold the vehicle registration document and MOT certificate? If not, why not?
△ Always arrange to view the car **in daylight** at the vendor's home – satisfy yourself it is **their** home.
△ **Never** allow them to bring the vehicle to your home or meet you at some other location.

GREATER MANCHESTER POLICE

TEXT 8

Jan de Vries Dutch Herbal Tea

Jan de Vries was born in Holland and trained as a pharmacist. His family has been involved in healthcare for many years, with his Grandmother being one of Holland's earliest herbalists.

During his thirty-five years in practise as a Naturopath, he has cared for many thousands of people from all over the world.

This Dutch Herbal Tea is part of a range of products formulated by Jan de Vries, designed to help you maintain a healthy life.

Jan de Vries *natural products for your health*

TEXT 9

We urgently need to answer more calls...

...and you can help without it costing you a penny

When children are crying out for help, someone needs to listen. And that's exactly what ChildLine does. ChildLine is the only free national helpline that provides **confidential comfort, help and protection** to young people in trouble or danger.

ChildLine works round the clock, answering over 3,000 calls daily. **But it's simply not enough.** BT, which logs attempted calls to ChildLine, tells us that up to 10,000 children try to call for help every single day. That means that thousands of children every day aren't getting the help they so desperately need. To ensure that ChildLine is there for every child, we must raise more funds... and with the **ChildLine Visa Card,** you can help us do just that, **at absolutely no extra cost to yourself.**

VISA

COMMENTARY All of the above nine texts are what might be called 'self-contained'. In other words though for inclusion here some have had to be shortened, they were all printed separately for distribution rather than appearing in a magazine or newspaper. They are typical of the trivia and junk mail that bombard all of us daily: mailshots; enclosures with letters and bills; sweet packets; public notices; leaflets delivered by hand or available in shops, libraries, etc.

You should not have found it difficult to identify the topic of each text, but in itself this tells you little. If the text is to have any chance of success the writer must consider the purpose of writing it and the target audience, in other words the particular people it is aimed at in society. Once clear about these aspects, the writer can concentrate on the best way of using language to achieve the desired effect.

In general terms all nine texts have been written to influence their target audiences in some way, but this statement is just a starting point. You will find that nearly all texts involve some degree of attempted influence – whether or not they are successful is quite another matter. Your list of purposes for the separate texts should be far more specific. You should be able to discover enough about the target audience in each case to enable you to draw up a profile. In turn, this profile should make it possible for you to identify some ways in which language is used that are appropriate to the specific purpose and audience.

To give you some idea of the degree of detail that you should be aiming for at this stage, an analysis of Text 7 follows.

1 *What is the text about?*
   The topic is the illegal sale of stolen second-hand cars to unsuspecting purchasers. (It is the front page of a four-page leaflet issued by Greater Manchester Police Vehicle Fraud and Autocrime Unit.)

2 *Why was the text written?*
   It was written to protect innocent purchasers from buying stolen vehicles.

3 *Who specifically did the writer intend should read the text?*
   Adults, generally though not exclusively drivers, who have little or no knowledge of the motor trade or car crime, who are likely to buy a car from an individual rather than a reputable dealer, and who are unaware of how to detect a suspect vehicle or vendor.

4 *In what way is the use of language different?*
   Here are some points:

■ The text is broken up into a number of smaller sections (introduction, research, etc) that in turn contain sentences spaced for ease of reading. A 'bullet point' arrangement is used with a triangle as an image of warning by analogy with road sign conventions.

■ There are variations in the size and style of font. These reflect the relative importance of the heading, sub-heading, or individual word. Certain words, for example, are emphasised by appearing in bold (eg **'identify'**, **'in daylight'**); some words appear in capital letters (known as upper case) as opposed to small (lower case).

■ The police force name and insignia at the bottom give authority to the contents and establish trust with the reader.

- The opening sentence is carefully chosen to contain dramatic facts delivered in a concise and impersonal manner.
- The bullet points resemble a list of organised instructions: the reader is either told what to do ('Decide', 'Find out', 'Consider') or is asked a question ('Can you identify...?', 'Does the vendor...?'). These help to organise the target audience as potential purchasers, supply relevant information, advise them, warn them, and provide clear and unambiguous instruction ('Always arrange', 'Never allow').
- Sentences, apart from the opening one, are quite short, ranging from 4 to 18 words; the average for the whole page is 11 words.
- The choice of vocabulary is not difficult to understand though it often avoids words that come to mind in speaking rather than writing (eg 'vendor' for 'seller', 'vehicle' for 'car', 'hold' for 'have'). The text manages to remain sufficiently formal and authoritative so that the target audience trusts it, yet also includes abbreviations that reduce formality (eg 'phone', 'adverts').
- The reader is regularly addressed as 'you' in order to maintain some personal contact between writer and target audience.

Several of the features identified are typical of leaflets, but it is important to identify clearly the specific ways in which language is used which contributes to the uniqueness of this text. In addition actual examples from the text have been provided as evidence in support of the points made. If you are going to examine a text, you must do it in a systematic way to ensure that your analysis is both comprehensive and complete. If your analysis of just some of the remaining eight texts is comparable in detail, you will be well on the way to developing a faculty for discriminating between different types of language use. The key concept you will by now appreciate is how much audience matters. A writer may have something to say, but unless they adapt their language to the profile of the target audience the message may never get through. The key question for a writer is not 'What do I want to say?' but 'How do I want to influence the reader?' This helps the writer focus on using language that is most likely to achieve this influence.

ACTIVITY 2

1 On your own, choose three of the remaining eight texts and analyse them in a similar way to the sample analysis of Text 7. Be sure to write down your findings and provide examples as evidence from each text.

2 Over the next week collect as many different examples of junk mail, free leaflets, flyers, etc as possible. These will provide a very useful resource to demonstrate some of the tremendous variety that exists in contemporary English and to exemplify techniques of current language usage. They will also prove helpful for later chapters of this book (eg Chapter 8 on advertising).

3 In small groups conduct a similar exercise with your collected texts to that carried out in Activity 1.

4 Alternatively, concentrate on just one from those you have collected and prepare a two-minute presentation in which you state clearly the topic, purpose and target audience, and identify some individual usage of language.

As a longer term project choose a topic or theme (eg crime, health, safety, flyers for clubs, local events) and collect as many texts as possible in order to discover the range and variety. Analyse each text and then write a short report summarising your findings, both similarities and differences. Did you find anything that was unexpected in the way language was used?

Register

So far you have discovered that the writing of any text depends upon the careful identification of topic, purpose and target audience, and that these crucial factors strongly affect (some would say dictate) the way in which the writer uses language. Any text contains features that make it different from others and which therefore allow you to identify it. When we refer to the individual way in which a text is written we speak of its **register**. The register of a text describes the way language expresses a specific topic aimed for a specific purpose at a specific audience. You can examine the register of any text with the confidence that you will uncover something about what makes it unique.

To develop a simple and effective system of enquiry you need to apply a set of useful questions that will reveal the details of a text's register. So far the questions comprising this framework for analysis may be summarised as follows.

What is the text about?	Topic: People, places, events, objects, ideas, facts, emotions, opinions, etc.
Why was the text written?	Purpose: To inform, persuade, warn, entertain, advise, instruct, reassure, encourage, report, remind, re-inforce, convince, etc.
Who is the text written for?	One person or many? What characteristics do they share in terms of age, sex, occupation, interests, knowledge, beliefs, values, culture, needs, aspirations, lifestyle, etc?
How is language used in the text?	In our analysis so far, we have covered five separate aspects (more follow in later chapters!):

1 Appearance: font type, style, size; use of symbols, logos, etc.
2 Overall structure: arrangement or shape of text (paragraphs, boxes, spacing, punctuation, etc).
3 Grammar: sentence type, length, complexity, etc.
4 Vocabulary: degree of familiarity or difficulty.

5 Tone: Manner in which the writer addresses the reader (friendly, personal, humorous, authoritative, sarcastic, etc).

This framework for analysis will be expanded to take account of the variety of texts discussed later in this book, but in its present state it is already quite a powerful instrument for text exploration. Before you apply this framework to some further data, you will find it helpful to familiarise yourself with another specific term in language study: **graphology**.

Graphology

Graphology is concerned with the appearance of the text – its layout and design – as opposed to the choice and meaning of the words; it therefore includes those aspects listed at **1** and **2** under the question 'How is language used?' It's as well to state here that like other subjects English Language has attracted a strikingly high number of specialist terms, many of which duplicate or overlap with others. Some authors use the term **graphetics** instead of graphology, but the latter is at present the more widely used. You should therefore be prepared to encounter alternative terminology in the wider reading you undertake later. This book will provide alternative terms only where they are widespread or likely to cause confusion.

Each text, then, has a register: a variety of language appropriate for its purpose. But there are some further complications! Have a look at the two texts below, both recipes for the same basic pie. Which one would you find easier to follow?

TEXT 10

CORNISH PASTIES

¼ lb raw meat • ¼ lb potatoes • ½ teasp. finely-chopped onion • mixed herbs to taste • salt and pepper • 2 tablesp. gravy *or* water • short crust pastry, using 8 oz. flour, etc.

Mince the meat finely. Dice the potatoes. Add the onion, herbs, salt, pepper, and gravy to the meat and potatoes, and mix well together. Divide the pastry into 8 equal portions and roll them out ¼ in. thick, keeping the portions as round as possible. Pile the mixture in the centre of each piece of pastry, wet the edges and join them together on the top to form an up-standing frill, prick them with a fork. Bake in a hot oven (**425°F., Gas 7**) for 10 min., then reduce heat to moderate (**350°F., Gas 4**) and cook for about 50 min. longer.

5–6 helpings

TEXT 11

Cornish pasty pie

(serves 6 people)

I find Cornish pasties often have too much pastry and not enough filling. However, the traditional filling of steak, potato and turnip is so delicious I now make one big pie using this filling – which is also a lot quicker than making individual pasties.

For the pastry:

6 oz lard (175 g)

12 oz plain flour (350 g)

Water to mix

Salt and freshly-milled pepper

For the filling:

1¼ lb chuck steak (560 g)

1 medium to large turnip

1 medium to large potato

1 large onion, finely chopped

½ teaspoon mixed herbs

1 tablespoon water

Salt and freshly-milled pepper

To glaze:

Beaten egg

Pre-heat the oven to gas mark 6, 400°F (200°C)

A well-greased 10 inch (25.5cm) fluted metal quiche tin.

Make the pastry first, adding a little salt and pepper to season it, then pop it into a plastic bag and leave it in the fridge for 10–15 minutes. Meanwhile, slice the meat into very thin strips about 2 inches (5cm) long (it's important to keep them very thin – in order that they cook in the time given).

Place the meat in a mixing bowl, with the chopped onion and mixed herbs. Then peel the potato and turnip and slice these as thinly as possible too (the slicing edge of a four-sided grater does this thin slicing job in moments). Now add the turnip and potato to the meat, season with salt and pepper, and mix very thoroughly.

Next roll out half the pastry, large enough to line the tin with about ½ inch (1cm) overlapping. Spoon the filling in, spreading it evenly all over, then sprinkle in 1 tablespoon of water.

Roll out the other half of the pastry, dampen the edge all round, then fit it over the top of the pie. Then seal the edges, folding them inwards and pressing gently to make a rim just inside the edge of the tin. Make a steam-hole in the centre (about the size of a 10p piece), brush the surface with beaten egg, and bake the pie on a baking sheet, on a high shelf, for 15 minutes. Then turn the heat down to gas mark 4, 350°F (180°C), and continue to cook on the centre shelf for a further ½ hours. This is still very good eaten cold, so it's a good idea for a picnic.

Unless you are a confident and accomplished cook you most probably preferred Text 11. A sensible response perhaps, but why exactly? To account for your choice you need to examine the many differences in the use of language between them. And you also need to be systematic.

ACTIVITY 4

1 In pairs, use the suggested framework of analysis to describe the particular register used in both recipes. You will find that the differences between the texts are explainable largely by an examination of the five aspects answering the question 'How is Language used?'. Don't forget to list examples from the text as evidence for your observations. (There is a suggested outline answer and commentary at the end of this chapter, but you should spend at least 15 minutes on this exercise before you look at them!)

2 In small groups discuss why you think the differences between the two texts exist. When do you think the two texts were written? What changes might have occurred within society during the period between them, and why have these brought about changes in language use?

COMMENTARY

This cookery lesson contrast reveals something else about texts. Despite the many differences in range and type of vocabulary, overall structure, and so on, both texts are clearly recipes. They therefore must share certain fundamental characteristics which enable you to recognise them. Examining the contrasts and their resulting effects has obviously been illuminating but there is a danger of overlooking an equally important fact. A particular type of text can undergo a degree of change in appearance and language, but can still retain its essential identity. Both texts use part of the vocabulary of cuisine, use commands in a logical sequence, and provide lists of ingredients separate from the instructions. However, they each display a distinct set of stylistic choices that neatly differentiates them. Some variation, a stylistic variation, can therefore exist between texts written in the same basic register.

ACTIVITY 5

Locate a pair of texts that are obviously of the same type but which contain contrasts in their use of language. One way to find such texts is by looking in magazines with similar content but aimed at different audiences in terms of age, sex, interest, etc. For example: horoscopes in *Family Circle* and *B*, the agony aunt page in *More* and *Company*, a health article in *Here's Health* and *Men's Health*, a fashion article in *Loaded* and *Marie Claire*, a cartoon strip in *The Beano* and *Viz*. Alternatively, you may be able to find similar texts in the same publication but separated by a period of time (at least ten years). List both the similarities and the differences, and suggest reasons for the differences. Consider how many of the similarities could undergo alteration without losing the essential character of the text.

ACTIVITY 6

A pair of contrasting texts on the same subject follows for analysis, either on your own or in pairs. Pay as much attention to the enquiry letter as to the reply.

TEXT 12

J-17
I THINK I'M GAY

I've never really been interested in boys. At first I thought it was just a phase, but it's been going on for so long that now I'm not sure. Whenever I see a pretty woman I feel attracted to her, but it feels wrong. I am quite scared. Please help.
Green Day fan (15)

Having feelings that seem 'wrong' can be scary. But let me assure you that there is absolutely nothing wrong with how you feel. Being attracted to members of the same sex is more common than you think, especially during puberty. Judging by my postbag, you are not alone in your confusion.

Whether or not this is 'just a phase' is another matter. It takes some people a while before they feel comfortable with their sexuality. They may even experiment before they figure out what feels right for them. In the meantime, try not to put so much pressure on yourself. There's no need to decide anything right now. If you'd like to talk to someone in confidence phone Careline on 0181–514–1177.

TEXT 13

Cosmopolitan

I am a 23-year-old confused girl. I have a steady relationship with my boyfriend, whom I've been with for three months, but recently, I've been feeling attracted to my own sex. A few years ago, I had a fling with a girl I met through a lesbian group. I love Pete and I don't know why I'm feeling this way again. My housemate knows how confused I am and, recently, has taken to wandering around in her undies. I don't want to do anything with her because I don't want to risk losing Pete. Also, I'm worried I may be misreading her signals. I can't talk to my family or friends about this. Could I be bisexual?

I'd tell your flatmate to put her clothes on, if I were you. You say she knows how you feel, but if you and she make love, you will be endangering your relationship with your boyfriend, unless you have serious feelings for her – in which case, what are you doing with him? Meanwhile, yes, it could be that you are lesbian or bisexual. Or, it could be that you are, for some emotional reason, unwilling to commit yourself to a heterosexual relationship. Or, could it be that, as much as you love your boyfriend, he is not altogether satisfying, sexually? Your best bet would be to contact a lesbian advice line or one of the 'Friend' lines that are listed in your local telephone directory – they do not exist to proselytise or to convert, but to advise.

COMMENTARY   Here is an outline answer and commentary on the recipes (Texts 10 and 11). Some of the features that you should have noted are:

TEXT 10

Graphology (including overall structure)

No variety in layout. A list of ingredients in paragraph one in bold font, each separated by just a dot. The instructions (or method) follow in one block paragraph using a small size of font with almost no variation in style and with very little space.

Grammar

Virtually no variation in sentence structure. Some are longer than others but they almost exclusively use verbs as commands: 'mince', 'dice', 'add', 'mix'. Little variation in links within sentences: mostly 'and'.

Vocabulary

A simple and unelaborated choice of words that does not fully explain the procedures: 'wet the edges', 'join them together'. Many abbreviations ('lb', 'teasp', 'tablesp', 'oz', 'in', 'min') likewise imply a degree of familiarity with cooking on the part of the reader.

Tone

Completely impersonal. No use of **colloquialisms** (see Chapter 3), that is, no words or phrases associated with spoken English of an informal variety. No expression of personal opinion by the writer.

Those are a few basic observations you might make after a few minutes in order to justify your initial reaction. This isn't by any means a comprehensive analysis, but already there is enough to make some interesting contrasts with Text 11.

TEXT 11

Graphology (including overall structure)

An introductory paragraph is followed by the necessary ingredients usefully subdivided. Paragraphing mirrors the separate stages of the recipe, making it user-friendly. Variety in layout is achieved by separate paragraphs, some inset. The font varies in style (standard, italic, bold, underline) and size. Space is used to improve readability and presentation.

Grammar

A mixture of sentences that are **statements** ('I find Cornish pasties often have …', 'This is still very good eaten cold …') or **commands** ('Make the pastry first …', 'Place the meat …'). Sentence structure is also varied – see for example the sentences with additional clauses within brackets. Links occur between sentences to indicate contrast and time sequence: 'However', 'Meanwhile', 'Then', 'Now'.

Vocabulary

A wider vocabulary with far greater description is provided: 'slice these as thinly as possible', 'dampen', 'seal the edges, folding them inwards and pressing gently'. Only the most common abbreviations are used: g for grams, cm for centimetres.

Tone

The writer identifies herself as 'I', thereby speaking to the reader. She uses a number of features associated with spoken rather than written language: 'a lot quicker', 'pop it', 'it's'; and adds information either as an afterthought: '– which is also a lot quicker than', or as a personal tip: '(about the size of a 10p piece)'. Notice how the use of punctuation devices such as the dash and brackets accentuate the informality. The whole piece is sprinkled with the writer's opinion – see particularly the opening paragraph and the concluding sentence – which identifies the writer as an individual. She is not an impersonal authority to be followed, but a human being who is pleased to pass on not only instructions but also tips and suggestions from her own experience.

You may well have noticed other features or examples, but you have now amassed quite a weight of evidence to show how Text 11 is simply easier to understand and follow. Mrs Beeton's authoritative tone, full of army type commands in basic language, will make you feel foolish if your pasty doesn't turn out perfect first time. Delia Smith is actually trying to help you cook.

And this leads to some further considerations about texts that will be developed in later chapters. Initially you might think of both texts as merely instructional in purpose. This is certainly true of Mrs Beeton's, but Delia Smith's also fulfils a number of subordinate yet highly important functions. She advises you about alternative approaches (paragraph 1) and on when and how to eat (cold on picnics); she encourages you to try the recipe ('is so delicious'); she explains processes in a way that supports your efforts. The text creates the illusion that you are following the advice of a professional speaking to you.

You have been introduced to stylistics by learning how to 'interrogate' texts by asking four basic questions:

- what is the text about?
- why was the text written?
- who is the text written for?
- how is language used in the text?

Further reading

Living Language by George Keith and John Shuttleworth. Hodder & Stoughton (1997). Chapter 7 contains a stimulating complementary introduction to varieties of language and text.

The Cambridge Encyclopedia of The English Language by David Crystal. CUP (1995). A book to browse and enjoy regularly.

2 Textbook Truth

In this chapter you will be exploring a number of extracts from non-fiction books that will enable you to develop an understanding of how texts are woven together in a variety of ways. In particular, you will consider the effects of choices made by the writer, consciously or otherwise, about grammar and vocabulary. You will then be able to appreciate the essential characteristics of the textbook, as well as the degree of variation in style that a writer can introduce.

What is a textbook?

If you were asked to list ten forms of popular or enjoyable reading, it is unlikely that you would include the textbook. As a type of writing it is seldom chosen for relaxation or pleasure. In some ways it is a strange name, for all books contain a text of one sort or another. Textbooks, however, traditionally contain a certain kind of text, one that will actually reveal much about the whole business of writing and register, if it is examined in the right way.

Admittedly, the material may not seem promising. A textbook is variously defined as 'A book containing the main principles of a subject' (*Chambers 20th Century Dictionary*, 1983), or 'A book used as a standard work for the study of a particular subject; a manual of instruction in a subject of study' (*The Shorter Oxford English Dictionary*, 1983). Such books are essential in the study of a vast number of subjects at progressively higher levels of difficulty. Indeed this very book you are reading is a form of textbook. By their nature they are classified as non-fiction, but not all non-fiction books are textbooks. The standard textbook tends to be written primarily for purposes of education or instruction rather than entertainment; it tends to be conservative in its view rather than controversial; it is comprehensive or detailed in its coverage, depending on the age, background and assumed level of knowledge shared by its target audience; its opinions and judgements will be rooted in facts. If a textbook deviated overmuch from this description it is unlikely that it would be bought in large enough numbers to be profitable for author or publisher. The extreme example of the textbook is the reference book, one normally established over time as the ultimate source for the 'true facts.' By contrast, many other non-fiction books rely upon their lightness of treatment or personal tone to entertain as much as to inform their readers.

Here is a complete chapter from a short book for young children about North American Indians.

TEXT 14

War

The Indian tribes fought with one another and with the white men who invaded their land. They fought with bows and arrows, knives, **lances** and **tomahawks**. Later they used guns sold by the white men. Over the years the white men took more and more Indian land. The Indians asked the government for help but were cruelly treated. This picture shows Cheyenne Indians being killed by General Custer's troops. The Indians later defeated Custer at the battle of the Little Bighorn. The small picture shows the famous Sioux chief Sitting Bull. He led his tribe into battle against the white men but could not stop the Indian lands being taken. After many battles the Indians were forced to live on **reservations**, far away from the plains that they loved.

The meaning in grammar

ACTIVITY 7

Before you read on, and without re-reading the above passage, write down in no more than twenty words a summary of its content. Compare this with your neighbour's and agree a combined version. You can continue this exercise until you have an agreed group or class version.

COMMENTARY

Text 14 fills two facing pages in the original and is accompanied by the two illustrations referred to. They depict cavalry soldiers attacking an Indian encampment, and Sitting Bull dressed in his chief's regalia. On a first reading you may not find anything particularly contentious here. It appears to be a suitably simplified and factual summary of the conflict that occurred between two cultures in the nineteenth century. It *seems* to present a true and accurate picture. However, if you look more closely, you will see considerable bias and factual distortion.

Two elementary but nonetheless important aspects of language choice can be examined here, one concerned with grammar, the other with vocabulary. Firstly, a crucial grammatical distinction can be made between sentences written in what is called the **active voice** as opposed to the **passive voice**. Many sentences can be written in either form, but the effect is different. Compare:

(a) The parrot pecked the sailor.
(b) The sailor was pecked by the parrot.

The same event is described in each sentence, but the emphasis in (a) is on the parrot pecking someone, whereas in (b) the emphasis is on the person being pecked. The verb 'pecked' in (a) is said to be active because it describes the action taken by the subject of the sentence, in this case the parrot. The parrot is the active participant, the **agent** or 'doer'. By contrast the verb 'was pecked' in (b) is said to be passive because the subject of the sentence, the sailor, is the passive participant. He takes no action but instead has something done to him. The contrast is between action and non-action.

Notice also that sentence (b) still makes perfect sense even if you omit the last three words. Using the passive construction means you don't have to identify who is responsible for doing the action. This can be a very useful option.

Applying this distinction to the text shows the emphasis given to events by the writer. As active participants, the Indians 'fought', 'used guns', 'asked', 'defeated', and 'loved'; Sitting Bull 'led' but 'could not stop'. By contrast as passive participants the Indians 'were (cruelly) treated', 'being killed', and 'were forced to live'; their lands were 'being taken'. The white men 'invaded' and 'took' (two aggressive actions) as active participants; they are not portrayed as passive participants. Note that although white men and Indians fight one another, only the latter are 'killed'. The cumulative effect is to present the Indians as warriors but ultimately victims, acted upon by the conquering and victorious white man. Sympathy is evoked for their fate, and this is emphasised by the choice of emotive words: they are 'cruelly' treated, and they end up 'far away' from the land they 'loved', this last verb describing a positive emotion denied to the white man.

Certainly the text contains facts, even though some of the content refers to imaginative illustrations rather than actual events. It summarises the conflict between two groups of people, but like much (some would say all) non-fictional writing, it carefully selects and presents facts so as to provide one particular viewpoint. It is not merely the choice of words that give meaning to the text, it is also the grammatical construction of those words. There's meaning in grammar.

ACTIVITY 8

1 As a group discuss the agreed version of your summary produced earlier. In the light of what you have now read, does it reflect any of the bias in the original source? To what extent does the original text contain opinion disguised as fact?

2 The apparent purpose of the text is to inform and educate young children about the lives of North American Indians. How has this discussion affected your perception of that purpose?

The meaning in words

The second important aspect of language choice concerns the individual words. The English language has an unusually varied and well-documented history that reflects the origins and travels of its speakers. Invasions of the British Isles by races during the first millennium AD, worldwide colonisation by the resulting nation during the second, have together created a language that now contains over one million words (no one knows the exact number, and in any case additions occur daily). Words have always been created or borrowed as the need arose. English is especially rich in **synonyms** – words that have the same or similar meaning. But this statement is misleading. Very few words mean *exactly* the same or are interchangeable in all contexts. Almost always there is some difference, however slight, such that substituting one word for another will alter the meaning in some way.

Some examples of apparent synonyms may make this clear. Three important sources of English words are Old English (the language spoken up until about 1100), French (the language spoken by the Norman conquerors and their descendants) and Ancient Greek and Latin (the languages of academic learning). Compare some words still in use today that derive from these sources:

Old English	French	Greek/Latin
ask	question	interrogate
eat	consume	ingest
fair	beautiful	pulchritudinous
fight	combat	hostilities
folk	people	nation
kingly	royal	regal
rise	mount	ascend
slow	tardy	dilatory
thin	pinched	emaciated

You will notice that the Old English words are short, simple, direct and commonly used. All but one here – 'kingly' – are **monosyllabic**, that is they contain one syllable. The French words are generally more formal or precise, longer and more literate; the Greek and Latin are abstract, technical, specialist and **polysyllabic** (containing several syllables). Often these differences reflect different registers: low and informal, polite and businesslike, or high and formal.

These distinctions are not unconnected with the three separate vocabularies that you possess. A **speaking vocabulary**, containing common everyday words that come to mind immediately and unconsciously; a **writing vocabulary**, containing words that you can call to mind after a little thought; and a **reading vocabulary**, consisting of words that you would normally be unable to bring to mind, but which you know and recognise when you see in print. You should not, however, equate these separate vocabularies with the origins of the words. Very many words of French origin are now extremely common, while many of Greek or Latin origin would perplex the most well-read of persons. For all that, the idea that you cannot access your total vocabulary with equal ease is significant.

Even a brief look at the vocabulary of the American Indian text reveals that the vast majority of words derive from Old English. The majority of most commonly occurring words in English come from this area, and so it should not be surprising that a book for young children contains such a high proportion.

ACTIVITY 9

1 On your own and with the help of a suitable dictionary, identify the origin of the verbs and nouns in the passage. Exactly how many are of Old English origin?

2 In pairs rewrite the passage by using words from a high register. You may need both a thesaurus and dictionary for this exercise! What is the effect of the changes?

COMMENTARY

Synonyms then are frequently not interchangeable. The three sentences 'My mate is bloody pissed', 'My friend is very drunk', and 'My companion is exceedingly inebriated' all mean essentially the same, though they obviously suit different occasions. However, there is a consistency in the choice of words making up each register, and if some elements are switched then the effect can be awkward or even humorous, eg 'My mate is bloody inebriated'. The unexpectedness of such a switch in registers is a device commonly used by comedians. Many short, simple, everyday words form part of what is sometimes called the **'core' vocabulary**: an essential fairly neutral set of words that occur comfortably in a wide range of contexts. Words like 'drunk', 'laugh', 'fat', 'mad', 'kill', 'dead'. They often have numerous synonyms that would be out of place in many situations. Compare for instance 'fat' with 'dropsical', 'obese', 'overweight', 'plump', 'bloated', and 'ginormous'.

ACTIVITY 10

1 Choose an example of a core word and in pairs write down as many similar words and phrases as you can. Then in larger groups or as a class compile a composite list.
2 Re-organise the words in your composite list under a number of headings according to similarity of register, for example slang or informal conversation; modern; dated or old-fashioned; literary; technical or specialist; negative and insulting; positive and complimentary. Note the variety of the total vocabulary that falls within the one semantic field (see p. 19), and the opportunities open to writers for creating different meanings. If you wish, you can now read the discussion of denotation and connotation in Chapter 5.

We can now make some further observations about vocabulary. Read the following extract from a history textbook for older children:

TEXT 15

Religion

The hold that religion had over people in the Middle Ages is almost unimaginable today. The power structure, centred on Rome, touched everyone. Even the King paid homage to his overlord the Pope. The archbishops of Canterbury and York directed the Church in their regions. There were two main types of clergy: seculars who took care of the spiritual interest of the lay people, and the religious orders who were full time worshippers, men and women who lived in monasteries and convents.

The parish priest played a vital role in the lives of ordinary people. He lived amongst them; baptized them when they came into the world; buried them in the churchyard when they left it. He often educated the children. In return, he was granted an extra strip of land and the people paid him tithes, a tenth of their assets.

Alternatively a priest might be employed by the local monastery, in which case he would be paid a salary. The first sort of priest was called a vicar, the second a rector, and the terms survive to this day.

COMMENTARY The first question to consider is 'What is the text about?' You will have no difficulty in discovering this, as the text is not difficult to understand, but where is the evidence if the heading 'Religion' is removed? The answer of course lies in the choice of words, in this case principally the nouns. Here are the main examples:

Nouns: 'religion', 'Pope', 'archbishops', 'Church', 'clergy', 'seculars', 'orders', 'worshippers', 'monasteries', 'convents', 'parish priest', 'churchyard', 'vicar', 'rector'.
Verb: 'baptized'.
Adjectives: 'spiritual', 'religious'.

These words make up a fundamental part of the text; without them the topic is missing. To return for a moment to our analogy with textiles, they represent an essential part of the particular pattern being woven by the author. By their regular appearance throughout, they act to hold the text together. This 'holding together' is referred to as **cohesion**, a word from Latin meaning simply 'sticking together'. Several types of cohesion are possible in composing a text; further examples will be examined in Chapter 3.

These words are all related; they each form a part of the total meaning involved in the word *religion*. In other words they all fall within the particular area or field of knowledge called religion. **Semantic field** is the term for a specific or defined area of knowledge or experience that is represented by related words and phrases. The term derives from **semantics**, the study of word meaning. Text 15 displays some of the words in the semantic field of religion. More specifically they are all related to the semantic field of Christianity, though a few (such as 'spiritual', 'religious') belong equally to other fields (eg Buddhism, Judaism).

Semantic fields can therefore be as large or small as is most useful. You can speak of the semantic field of colour, which includes: *hue, pigment, brilliance, shade, luminosity, tint* and *red;* or the semantic field of red, which includes: *crimson, vermilion, scarlet, geranium, ruby, blush, rouge,* and *robin redbreast.*

More intricate texts frequently display the interweaving of a number of semantic fields, so as to add interest and variety for the reader.

ACTIVITY 11

In pairs or small groups re-examine Text 2 or 3 in Chapter 1 (see p 2).
1 What semantic fields can you identify?

2 How do they contribute to the meaning and overall effect of the text?

ACTIVITY 12

Turn back to the two recipes in Chapter 1 (see pp 8–9).
1 List the words and phrases from the semantic field of cookery in each.

2 What difference do you detect between them?
3 How does this contribute to the perceived difference in effect?

Reading texts

When reading any text it is important to suspend judgement on it until you fully understand exactly what the writer is saying. One way to discover this is by distinguishing three separate stages in reading:

1 **Reading to Understand**
   What is the writer saying? The answer often involves checking word meanings and references.
2 **Reading to Interpret**
   What does the writer mean by what they say? What is the writer's personal argument or opinion?
3 **Reading to Evaluate**
   How can the writer's view be criticised? How much is fact or opinion? What evidence is included?

You will be familiar with these three stages as a strategy for comprehension of a text. In practice, you can often perform all three simultaneously. However, the more demanding the text, the greater the need to slow down the process. By placing an increasing emphasis on how language is used, you transform this elementary approach into a powerful framework of questions that allows you to comprehend and criticise at a much deeper level.

This next extract, from a textbook for secondary schools about the place of women in history, sets out to inform the reader about the way in which women were perceived in medieval society.

ACTIVITY 13

1 Read the text carefully. Refer to the framework of questions in Chapter 1 (see p 7).
   a In pairs identify the topic of the text by reference to the semantic fields included.
   b Write down what you consider to be fact and what you consider to be opinion.
2 Now examine how language is used in the extract.
   a In particular look at the choice of vocabulary and the semantic fields that it represents. How do the vocabulary and the semantic fields chosen indicate the writer's personal attitude towards the topic?
   b What purposes do you think the writer had in mind when writing this text?
3 In groups compare your separation of fact from opinion, and your identification of semantic fields and writer's purposes. Are you able to agree on your responses?

TEXT 16

There was yet another powerful influence on the ideas held about women in the Middle Ages. This was the romantic conception of the remote, and adored, lady-love for whom knights and squires rode forth to gain honour and renown. The poetry of the age is full of this visionary being and there is a reason for this. Marriage in those days was a bargain between parents for material gain. Child marriages were common. Much of the Church teaching on marriage was, as we have seen, mundane, so men sought for romantic love outside their marriage. The mere thought of everyday intimacy was distasteful and they preferred to worship from afar. This idealistic treatment of women was harmful, in that it was unrealistic, but perhaps it did help to make men gentler and more respectful to women in general.

COMMENTARY Text 16 highlights the effects possible in choice of noun, adjective and verb to construct a cohesive text with a particular purpose and viewpoint. In terms of grammar you will have noticed the frequent use of the past tense of the verb 'to be'. The effect of this is to make what the writer says appear to be true or certain. 'Was' or 'were' occur eight times, indicating a certainty of fact; 'is' occurs twice, and seems even more convincing. The only suggestion of doubt is contained in the use of 'perhaps', though arguably this is neutralised by the following emphatic 'did'. Of course, you would expect incontrovertible facts to be reported in such an indisputable way. On the other hand, such a technique is clearly open to abuse.

Another fundamental and telling aspect of grammar is that all the sentences in Text 16 are statements, as opposed to questions, commands or exclamations. Statements (or **declaratives**), as their name implies, state or declare something rather than question it. They are by far the most common sentence type, and you might well predict that they will predominate in textbooks. The other less frequent but just as useful sentence types are the question or **interrogative**, that asks something, the command or **imperative**, that orders someone, and the **exclamation**. For example:

Declarative:	Ivan loves lobster.
Interrogative:	Does Ivan love lobster?
Imperative:	Eat that lobster today.
Exclamation:	What a tasty lobster!

The following extract is from *Beginning Psychology* by M Hardy and S Heyes, an introductory textbook aimed at GCSE students and above.

TEXT 17

A study performed by Philip Zimbardo of Stanford University in the USA shows, in a startling fashion, how people can become locked into roles from which they find it difficult to escape. Volunteers were asked to play the role of the prisoner or guard, and were assigned one of the roles randomly. They were taken to a 'jail' and asked to play their role. The 'prisoners' were stripped and deloused and given prison clothing to wear. They were given numbers instead of being allowed to use their names. Guards were given uniforms, truncheons and sunglasses. Concealed cameras filmed what happened next. Although the simulation was supposed to run for 14 days, it had to be stopped after only six days, as both prisoners and guards were so locked into their roles that the guards made prisoners clean out toilet-bowls with their bare hands, or force-fed them, or put them in solitary confinement. The prisoners, far from fighting the guards, became apathetic and subservient and allowed the guards to do what they wished. The guards at their debriefing after the simulation were very surprised at how cruel they had been, but several mentioned that they had felt that they were locked into their role to such an extent that it overcame their normal moral aversion to behaving cruelly towards other people.

ACTIVITY 14

1 Either on your own or in pairs examine the text. In terms of register, what can you say about its use of language and tone? In particular you might note the occasions where passive sentences occur, and comment on the reasons for this and their effect.

2 On your own rewrite the text completely in the active voice. What is the effect of this change?

3 Discuss as a large group or class the problems in performing this rewriting exercise.

Here are two texts that discuss the same topic, abortion, but in very different ways. You will no doubt sense this difference, but you are now learning how to discover why you respond in a certain way.

TEXT 18

ARTIFICIAL ABORTION

It need hardly be said that nothing must be done to interfere with pregnancy should it have already occurred. The moment that fertilisation takes place, the development of the living child is begun, and any interference causes its death. As can be readily understood, such an act is legally criminal, and no qualified doctor would be a party to such a procedure. There are certain very rare cases where two or three doctors consulting together may consider it right to empty the womb, but such cases are so rare that they need not be considered.

There are, however, any number of non-medical people who make a trade of the surgical production of abortion; this interference often causes the gravest risk to health, and women not infrequently die as the result of it. In view of this danger to the mother's health, as well as of the fact that these practices are illegal, no person should have resource to unqualified people.

Certain forms of drugs for the purpose of 'getting rid' of an early pregnancy are unfortunately quite easy to obtain in the shops, and the laws governing the sale of these seem to be much too lax. A woman may quite likely injure herself gravely by using them, and an abortion has always an unfavourable effect on a woman's health, often making her nervously run down for a long period.

PRACTICE ABROAD

There are countries where abortion is legalised, but there the tendency is to give less care and attention to methods of birth control, knowing that the woman can have an operation performed if she becomes pregnant. It is much better that people should rely on contraceptives, and women are strongly advised to pay attention to the proper use of such methods, so that they will indeed prove secure, which they can be, if the directions here given are carefully followed and the appliances carefully stored, kept in good condition, and renewed when necessary.

TEXT 19

ABORTION

For many women abortion is a positive choice. Having an abortion can be much less traumatic physically and emotionally than having an unwanted child. The safest and easiest time to have an abortion is within the first three months (first trimester) of the pregnancy.

This is the first time I really told people because it was such a big thing for me. There are so many women who've had abortions. These women have made these choices, too – so nothing's wrong with me ... When you are willing to talk about it, it makes another feel she can talk to you.

I was the mother of three little boys. Being a mother and having children has always been very important to me, and this made the decision that much more difficult. Loving children as I do, I also knew that having the baby and then giving it up for adoption would not be an option for me.

My lover was opposed to having the child (as a team) and I didn't want another child without his help, so I decided on abortion. I was not happy with this because I wanted the child and was in love with the father.

I knew that abortions were legal, but that's all. I was afraid to mention it to my doctor. I thought he'd accuse me of being evil. (He didn't.) I also thought I'd be in terrible pain. He explained the procedure the day before. It was very helpful.

I get so bitter hearing people piously stating how those poor babies have a right to live and there are lots of people who want babies and can't have them. A baby isn't just produced and given away and that's that. You're talking about a part of a woman's body. That baby is part of her, and to expect her to give it up after going through a pregnancy is really ridiculous. I know many women could, but many couldn't. I couldn't have. I know that without my abortion I would have gone through nine months of hell, dealing with my boyfriend, my parents, my friends, my job, my financial situation, my health, my whole future and then thinking about the baby, its future, would I keep it or not, how to support it, and so on – one headache after another. At that time in my life, I don't think I could have handled it all. I couldn't even handle it now, and I'm better off now than I was a year ago.

1 Remind yourself of the framework questions on page 7. Then read through both texts and write answers to the following questions. Be as specific as you can and give reasons for your answers.

a When (roughly) do you think each text was produced?

b In exactly what sort of publication would you expect to find each one?

c What can you work out about the background of each writer?

d What kind of reader did each writer have in mind?

e Does either text contain any features of spoken language?

f What do you think is the purpose of each text?

g Would you include yourself in the target audience of either text?

h How do you personally respond to each text?

Remember that you must suspend your personal reaction to each text if you are to fully understand it. In other words, you have to recognise that your instinctive like or dislike for a particular text may not be the most important standard by which to judge it!

2 In small groups compare your responses. Agree on a group response to each question.

3 Discuss the differences in the way the two writers use language. One member in each group should be responsible for recording your findings. Make sure you find specific examples from the texts to support your observations.

4 Individually, rewrite the first paragraph of Text 18 in a modern-day register suitable for persons of your own age and background. Compare your version with your neighbour's.

Text types

In this chapter you have examined examples of textbooks that vary in their use of language depending on their topic, their target audience, and when they were written. What features do they share that allow them to be grouped together? Perhaps it is a question of fact over opinion, truth over fiction, impersonal tone as opposed to personal? Are these distinctions clear-cut or are they merely a matter of emphasis? There are no simple answers to these questions.

Texts that are sufficiently similar to one another can be conveniently grouped together into what is called a **genre**, a word derived from Latin and meaning 'kind' or 'type'. A genre can be defined as a grouping together of texts that share some significant features. Traditionally, this organisation of text types into categories has been one way of dividing up the world of literature, the three main genres being drama, poetry and prose. However, these genres are so large and general as to be at times unhelpful. It can be more useful to subdivide each into smaller sub-genres. So, for instance, drama can be broken down into tragedy, comedy, black comedy, farce, kitchen-sink, melodrama, and so on. Likewise the genre of TV entertainment can be subdivided into soap, sitcom, game show, chat show, etc. This sounds very neat and precise until you realise that overlap can occur: some drama can be written in poetry (poetic drama) or be a mixture of two sub-genres (tragi-comedy). Nevertheless, the idea of being able to classify texts according to similarities has advantages, among them the fact that you have a fairly clear idea of what to expect before you begin watching a soap or a farce.

The boundaries between the various genres and sub-genres may be slightly fuzzy, but that need not worry you at the moment. Genres in any case are constantly evolving and borrowing from one another, an aspect that is discussed in later chapters. At this stage, it is more important to appreciate the distinguishing features that each genre shares. Two significant features are topic (the subject matter or theme) and general structure (including visual appearance as well as grammar and choice of vocabulary). A simplified diagram or 'genre-tree' shows the relationship:

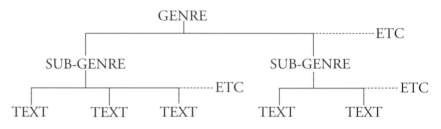

The individual texts are likely to share a number of more detailed features of register, though there will also be stylistic differences (see the discussion of the two recipes in Chapter 1).

ACTIVITY 16

In groups, look again at the textbook extracts in this chapter. Discuss whether they all fall under the heading of a 'textbook' genre, or is it possible to divide them into a number of sub-genres? You may not arrive at a final agreement, but it is more important to understand the differences of opinion. You may decide that one feature of the textbook is that the reader is not explicitly addressed. The book you are reading would, however, contradict this finding. On your own over the next week or so look for as many different types of textbook as you can. Summarise their distinctive features in note form (with examples).

ACTIVITY 17

1 Collect lots of examples of a particular type of non-literary text, eg, flyers, e-mails, classified personal ads, answer-phone messages, receipts, and 'blurbs' on book covers.

2 Analyse the register of each and draw up a list of similarities and differences.

3 Either write a short report in which you justify the grouping together of all your chosen texts as one sub-genre, or make a short presentation of your findings to a small group.

In this chapter you have learnt about the effects of using the active or the passive voice; the importance of semantic fields in contributing to the overall meaning and cohesion of a text; and you have been introduced to the concepts of genre and sub-genre.

Further reading

Rediscover Grammar by David Crystal. Longman (1996). An extremely user-friendly publication that clearly explains basic grammar in bite-sized chunks.

Semantics by F R Palmer. CUP (1981). Still an excellent little introduction.

English Words by F Katamba. Routledge (1994). A more comprehensive, but popular and readable text.

3 The Unreadable Voice

In this chapter you will investigate some of the differences between speech and writing. You will also examine a wide range of texts that demonstrate the way writers and speakers manipulate the features of spoken and written language to their advantage.

Speaking or writing

What's the difference? Well, after a moment's thought you would probably say that there are differences, that you generally don't write in the same way as you speak. But what exactly are these differences? How important are they? And what relevance do they have to the analysis of texts?

A simple starting point for investigating this topic is to examine a typical example of speech:

TEXT 21

Right so you're coming up the M61? right well er you're looking for er the sign for signs for Preston not not the first one cos that's for south Preston an' you don't want that OK? (.) when you see that you get you get into the other lane (.) for Preston er and Lancaster I think an' you stay in that till you join the M6 (.) it's not far (.) er then er you need to it's pretty busy there you've got to change lanes sometimes cos of all the traffic coming up behind you but (.) anyway you need to get into get back into the left hand lane so you can come off at the turn-off (.) junction (2) er dunno the number but it it's signed for the A59 Preston (1) an' er Clitheroe you know but you want the Preston first exit (.) right well you go up the hill right? an' you oh you gotta be kinda careful there (.) there's speed restrictions there now er the bill's often lurking up there with the old infra-red gun thing to catch you (.) I almost got er don't get caught! (1) anyway you go up the hill (.) you 'member that pub by the cemetery where we met that time? (.) you know on Blackpool Road (.) well you reach that the (.) the round-about's there.

Seeing in print the actual words that somebody used in speaking to communicate with someone else is always a revelation. There are no misprints in the extract! If you are unused to seeing transcripts of real speech, you will have found it hard to read and understand. Note that the parentheses signs () indicate a pause, either short with a full stop (.) or longer with the number of seconds, eg (2).

ACTIVITY 18

1 In pairs examine Text 21 and list as many features as you can that make it so obviously spoken rather than written language. Write down as many reasons as you can for these differences. Suggested answers to this activity can be found at the end of the chapter. Read them only after you have attempted it yourself.

2 Rewrite the extract as part of a set of written instructions.
   a How would your rewriting differ if you were writing a letter to a friend rather than a set of instructions to motorists?
   b What difficulties did you face in attempting this task?
   c Why is it not simply a matter of repunctuating the passage?

The relevance of speech

If spoken language is so very different from written language then how can it be relevant to the examination of written texts? Well, may be different but that doesn't mean that the two varieties of expression never meet and mix. Certainly in the more politically and economically developed parts of the world today, the written form of a language carries far greater status. There is a stigma attached to 'illiterate' people who can neither read nor write. Our education system teaches us that the best writing is carefully planned and well-organised, it is corrected and revised, it is explicit and precise. An economy of expression is considered a virtue.

By comparison speech appears a very poor relation. And yet it is unfair to apply the principles and conventions of writing to spontaneous speech. The average person simply does not, and for the most part cannot, speak in grammatically complete and concise sentences. It is for this reason that in writing we call the basic unit of expression (and therefore of analysis) the sentence, and in speech the utterance. You write in sentences; you speak in utterances. Speech and writing are two different mediums and are suited to different purposes. Speech for instance is often preferred for communicating things of a more informal, personal or intimate nature, whereas writing is reserved for formal or abstract matters.

ACTIVITY 19

1 On your own compile a list of:
   a occasions when you would communicate by speech only
   b occasions when you would communicate by writing only
   c occasions when either option would be acceptable, though you might personally prefer one to the other.
2 Next in pairs or small groups discuss your three categories. Do you agree? Choose one or two examples from c and discuss what differences in language there would be between the spoken and written versions.
3 Choose one example from c and write out both the written and spoken versions. Then write a paragraph in which you compare the crucial differences.

More recently many of the traditional distinctions between the written and spoken word have become somewhat blurred. The mediums frequently borrow from each other to achieve certain effects. Advertisers (see Chapter 8) among others will deliberately write ads that incorporate features of spoken language in order to project an image of informality or friendliness. On the other hand, public speakers will spend much time planning and crafting speeches, both to remove many of the more distracting features of speaking, as well as to consider carefully the likely effect of their words.

1 In pairs re-examine texts 2 and 6 on pages 2 and 3. How many features of spoken language have been included in these texts? What is their likely effect on the target audience and how might this alter if those features were removed?

2 As a longer term assignment collect as many examples of answer-phone messages as you can. Transcribe (write down) the messages and examine them for aspects of spoken and written language.

3 After a fortnight these can be brought in for class discussion. In small groups you should examine them for any patterns you detect in their structure. Then write out a message suitable for a machine:
   a at your home
   b at your school, college or place of work.
   What differences exist between the two?

Here is the opening of a political speech made by William Hague, when Leader of the Conservative Party, at the close of the Party Conference on 10 October 1997. This is an excellent example of a text that has been carefully written to be spoken.

TEXT 22

I said that I wanted a fresh conference. I believe that this week we have had the freshest and most constructive and exciting conference for years. I said that I wanted an open conference. This week we have had some of the most open and vigorous and honest debates that any party has had for years and years. I said that I wanted a clear conference. And this week the message of change and renewal has come out of this hall with a clarity and directness rarely seen in modern politics. I said that I wanted a united conference. There is no doubt that this week you have demonstrated a new unity of purpose and a new unity of conviction that none of the pundits predicted. Fresh, open, clear and united. That is what I wanted to see and that is what this conference has delivered.

The only long faces in the hall have been those of the vultures who came to pick over the carcass of the Tory Party. I don't want anybody to leave this hall disappointed. But when it comes to the vultures, I'm delighted to make an exception. Far from being dead we have embarked on a process of reform and renewal that will rebuild our party, rejuvenate our membership, restore our confidence and make us fit to return to govern at the next General Election.

And I'll tell you something else: we made a bit of history here this week. I am the first Conservative Leader to have been able to welcome to our conference three former Leaders of our party, each one of whom served this country as its Prime Minister. Last week, Tony Blair welcomed three of his predecessors to his conference in Brighton. Only one of them had served as Prime Minister – let's be thankful for that. And that is the ratio I intend to maintain. Of course, it is important for a new Leader to take advice from his predecessors as all three of mine often tell me.

But advice can be a two-way street. As some of you may remember, I gave a speech in this very hall 20 years ago almost to the day. I told Margaret Thatcher what she had to do to be a successful Prime Minister. I suppose it was a bit presumptuous, but you've got to admit – it worked! And you have to hand it to her, she took the message to heart. I spent three minutes telling Margaret what she needed to do. Then, to the lasting benefit of this country, she spent the next 13 years telling all of us what to do.

1 In pairs read the above extract carefully. How can you tell that it has not been delivered spontaneously? Draw up two lists, one to include typical features of everyday speech absent from the text, and one to include those that are present.

2 Discuss and write down in note form the answers to three of the basic questions relating to register: What is the text about? Why was it written? And who was it written for?

3 As a class or large group share your findings

and discuss the reasons for the exclusion or inclusion of such features. Remember that you cannot be sure of the ultimate success or failure of the speech, as in any case this must in some part depend on the speaker himself. Similarly, you are not debating the truth or otherwise of the content. Your focus must be on why language has been used in a certain way. You can then debate why you think these choices of language use might or might not have been effective.

Developing the analysis system further

COMMENTARY Your discussion of the Hague speech should have included some comments on grammar, vocabulary and tone, all of which were introduced in Chapter 1. Each of these needs to be expanded for incorporation into the framework of analysis that you are using. In other words, you need to develop your knowledge about language so that in turn you become increasingly skilled at criticising a text. Here are some observations that can be applied to future textual analysis.

Grammar

Several of the early sentences contain an identical opening: 'I said that I wanted . . .'. The conclusion of each also displays a very similar pattern: 'a fresh conference', 'an open conference', 'a clear conference', 'a united conference'. This device is referred to as **syntactic parallelism**, in other words, the repetition of a grammatical structure that appears to run in parallel with another. Its intended effect, like so many contrived techniques of language use, is to emphasise and reinforce the meaning in some dramatic or memorable way. A sense of balance is experienced from hearing the text, strengthened by the recurrence of the rhythms in the similar structures. You will notice further examples in the second, fourth, sixth and eighth sentences, though these contain slightly more variation to prevent predictability and monotony. The next two sentences underline and summarise what Hague has just said by further repetition of the key words.

This type of patterning can occur within a sentence as well as between sentences. The sentence beginning: 'Far from being dead . . .' contains the clauses 'rebuild our party', 'rejuvenate our membership', 'restore our confidence', and 'make us fit to return', the last again being an attempt to add variety to the phrasing.

Phonology

Phonology is the study of the system of sounds used in a particular language. Traditionally it is also applied to the manner in which certain combinations of sounds are produced for effect (eg **rhyme, alliteration, assonance**). The sentence beginning 'Far from being dead . . .', for instance, exemplifies an alliterative pattern in its deliberate use of initial 're' sound in six words, stressing further both the rhythm and the meaning.

Vocabulary

Words and phrases have been chosen to project a dynamic and forward-looking image: 'fresh', 'open', 'vigorous', 'clear', 'united', 'renewal', 'rejuvenate', 'benefit'. Some adjectives recur in a superlative form ('freshest', 'most open'), others recur as nouns linked to equally positive ideas ('clarity' and 'directness', 'unity of purpose', 'unity of conviction'). A large proportion of these nouns and noun phrases are **abstract** and general rather than **concrete** and particular, and this tendency recurs throughout (eg, 'process of reform and renewal'). Nouns are also modified by vague yet highly positive and forceful adjectives: 'freshest and most constructive and exciting conference', 'most open and vigorous and honest debates'). The cumulative impression is of a serious speaker who is supremely confident and certain about his ideas for the future.

Tone

The observations on vocabulary have already provided some evidence for the tone of the text. As a leader responsible for policy it is appropriate that Hague should refer to himself (as 'I') regularly, but he also frequently uses 'we' to include himself with his supporters in order to demonstrate joint solidarity in the Party's shared beliefs and goals. He thus avoids the danger of appearing too authoritarian or distant. Choice in use of pronouns is a key aspect when reviewing the tone of a text. A writer or speaker cannot help but betray his attitude to his target audience by his use or avoidance of these so significant words. Although his vocabulary is fairly formal and serious sounding, he does occasionally introduce a colloquialism when he appears to be sharing a sentiment with his audience: 'And I'll tell you something else . . .', 'let's be thankful for that . . .', 'I suppose . . . but you've got to admit – it worked!' Having mentioned a previous Prime Minister by her full name, he subsequently refers to her merely as 'Margaret'. These lighter touches attempt to give some intimacy to a text that might otherwise sound too monotonous in its style of delivery.

In Chapter 2 the concept of cohesion was introduced as one means that a writer uses to link a text together. Cohesion there was achieved by choices in vocabulary, but other types exist. In addition to using certain patterns of vocabulary, Hague also uses patterns of grammar, and patterns of phonology in the sound and rhythm of language. Cohesion can therefore be also grammatical and phonological. Traditionally, **rhetoric** was the term used to describe skills in persuasive speaking, which would include the devices that Hague uses. A more useful term for any individual device in language study is **foregrounding**: any use of language that is in some way unusual in context so as to attract attention. The term comes from painting, in which the artist places the more significant objects nearer to the viewer than those in the background. Hague attempts to foreground his meaning by establishing patterns of word choice, of repetitive grammatical structure, of rhythm and alliteration. Analysis is very much concerned with the discovery of such patterns. It is a search, if you like, for the individual 'stylistic fingerprints' of a writer.

Note that these observations form the first part of an analysis that describes textual features and explains their intended effects. This is not the same as evaluating whether or not the text is good or bad, effective or otherwise.

Only when you have completed a comprehensive and detailed analysis are you in a position to comment on the value or effectiveness of a text. If you judge a text prematurely, say for instance on the basis of your own political beliefs, your subsequent analysis will inevitably be selective rather than extensive, biased rather than open-minded, and subjective not objective.

ACTIVITY 22

As a class prepare and debate whether you believe that William Hague uses language effectively in the opening of his Party Conference speech.

Some components of language

Language is undoubtedly a highly complex instrument for communication. In order to explore its use in texts it can prove helpful to break it down into smaller chunks. There are several ways of doing this, but one way is to separate it into three more manageable areas of study.

As a tool for communication, language has a certain form and structure. You produce a set of sounds that you organise in a particular way in order to communicate meaning. In the more developed parts of the world this meaning can alternatively be written down as well as spoken. Whichever medium is used, the language system needs agreed rules about the structure of words, utterances and sentences so that (theoretically) no misunderstanding occurs among the users of the language. Language can be described as 'a rule-governed system'.

Each individual language is unique in the set of sounds (phonology) or letters and punctuation (graphology) that it uses to create units of meaning (words or vocabulary) which it arranges in uniquely organised structures (grammar). It will be obvious that this description is simplified, but nonetheless it summarises three essential components of the form that language takes: its phonology and graphology, its vocabulary, and its grammar. In examining a text it can be less daunting if at the outset you tackle each of these components separately, before you fit them together in a consolidated summary. You will notice from now on that this book often uses the word **lexis** rather than vocabulary. Essentially there is no difference between them, but you should become familiar with the shorter word as it is now firmly established in language studies.

You are accumulating a number of technical terms connected with the study of language. These will prove increasingly useful and necessary as you develop confidence in examining and discussing texts. In fact, without such terms it becomes hard to talk in a precise and detailed way about them. Any subject needs a collection of specialist terms – a terminology or 'jargon' – in order to describe concepts and clarify thinking. The jargon provides a valuable shorthand between people interested in the same subject. In the case of English studies you need a specialist language in order to talk in a meaningful way about language.

The following is the opening of a speech given by the headmaster of an independent primary school at the Annual General Meeting attended by governors, staff and parents. Names have been omitted in the interests of confidentiality.

TEXT 23

Mr Chairman, Governors, Ladies and Gentlemen, good evening and welcome to our AGM and Governors' Election and a special welcome to those new parents of [school name] for whom this is their first attendance at our yearly meeting. I trust that you will all find the proceedings enlightening as well as enjoyable. My task at this occasion is to put before you a résumé of the activities at school during the last academic year. This I shall certainly do – for it would be greatly remiss of me to allow the year to fade into obscurity without my remarking upon its noteworthy achievements. However, I hope I shall be excused if, in the pursuance of an alternative perspective, I concentrate my thrust this evening as much on the future as on the past.

Anyone who has read the most recent edition of [school magazine] will, I am sure, not only attest to the superlative quality of the magazine and its contents, but will also not have failed to have been left with an impression of [school name] as a purposeful, dynamic, enlightened and progressive educational establishment. The magazine is replete with all the school's achievements, successes (and a few failures) in every enterprise and endeavour with which the school has embarked upon. It permeates an impression of life and liveliness, pride and passion, delectation and (I hope) devotion. The philosophy and ethos of the school and the high expectations of our pupils and the quality of education they receive – in the broadest sense – are enshrined on the pages of that document which is a testament to the quality of teaching which exists within the school and which is perpetuated year on year. I am greatly indebted to all its contributors, but in particular [name] for his editorial expertise in compiling a journal of such excellence.

ACTIVITY 23

1 Read the extract carefully. In groups identify the specific features of language in the text, paying particular attention to the choice of vocabulary. What are the characteristics of this register?

2 On your own, rewrite the extract making any changes to vocabulary and grammar that you feel might be appropriate for the target audience.

3 Then write a paragraph explaining in what ways you have altered the register, and how you think this would affect the target audience.

The following is an extract from Professor Jean Aitchison's fifth 1996 BBC Reith Lecture on language entitled 'A World-wide Web'.

TEXT 24

Persuasion is of course a major use of language, maybe one of its original uses. Everyone needs to be on their guard. Overt mind-bending is usually easy to detect. Advertisements go in for **obvious** mind-bashing, and the speakers at speakers' corner are **clearly** trying to influence us. But less direct persuasion may trap the unwary. Language worries **worth** worrying about **do** exist. They rarely appear to be major perils, but like a banana skin, or a loose paving stone, they can trip people up, and cause more damage than might be foreseen. A single strand in a spider's web might at first catch a fly by one leg, but then entrap it further. Speakers therefore need to watch out. If they clear their minds of pseudo-worries, such as anxiety about split infinitives, then they might have more energy left to notice these genuine pitfalls.

The 'gobbledegook' syndrome is the most straightforward of these snares. Gobbledegook can be defined as pretentious or unintelligible jargon, as when a young man impresses others with 'idle chatter of a transcendental kind' in Gilbert and Sullivan's opera *Patience*. Gobbledegook needs to be 'translated' into comprehensible language – though it must not be confused with **technical** vocabulary. A doctor talking to another doctor might justifiably use words such as electroencephalography or mesenteric adenitis. However, medical terms **can** become gobbledegook if used inappropriately: 'Is there any history of cardiac arrest in your family?' a doctor asked. 'We never had no trouble with the police,' was the indignant reply.

Politically correct terms are sometimes labelled gobbledegook. But this is not entirely justified. The PC movement has some beneficial spin-offs. 'Firefighter' or 'bar-person' in an ad makes it clear that either sex can apply. The PC movement is still young, and some PC phrases sound very bureaucratic, as with 'visually challenged' for 'blind', or 'developmentally inconvenienced' for older 'mentally retarded'. But PC hearts are in the right place, even if their tongues or pens are twisted up in sesquipedalian words.

ACTIVITY 24

Write a full analysis of the extract, paying particular attention to the ways that the speaker uses language to hold the listener's attention. Use the framework for analysis questions to provide a structure for your answer, and add a conclusion in which you assess the relative success or otherwise of the speaker.

Degrees of formality

Different situations call for varying degrees of formality, in language just as much as in personal dress or behaviour. You need to develop your critical powers beyond a vague assertion that a text is rather formal or rather informal. Imagine that you are travelling somewhere by rail. At various points on your journey you may be challenged to prove that you have actually bought a ticket.

1 You may be still waiting for the train when you catch sight of a notice fixed to the wall which in large bold upper case letters reads:
 ALL TICKETS MUST BE SHOWN
2 You board the train and hear a number of announcements over the intercom system including:
 'Customers are requested to have their tickets ready for inspection.'
3 A few minutes later a conductor approaches you:
 'Do you have your ticket, sir?'
4 You change trains at Crewe and again are no sooner seated when:
 'Got a ticket?'
5 And finally, you reach your destination, not believing that your now grubby ticket will be needed further, but at the barrier:
 'Ticket, mate?'
 And you hand it over.

Now essentially the same meaning is conveyed by all five communications, but they certainly vary in their respective levels of formality, and during the course of the journey they also become progressively less and less formal. So far so good. But how do you actually know that they differ from one another in this way?

ACTIVITY 25

In pairs identify exactly what it is about the arrangement and choice of words in each sentence or utterance that causes you to rank them in a descending order of formality. You should do this before reading the following notes.

COMMENTARY Some of the features you might have identified are:

1 A declarative sentence, but one that demands compliance without exception: 'all' and 'must'. It is completely impersonal, the focus being on the tickets rather than the persons who bought them. This impersonality is further emphasised by the passive construction of the sentence. It is obviously one-way communication, the notice being there to inform or remind travellers of an obligation.
2 Again a declarative sentence making a statement, but one that suggests a

precise and polite compliance in its use of the more formal 'requested' as opposed to the simpler 'asked'. It is not absolutely impersonal, as people are addressed in the plural as a group by 'Customers' and 'their'; again the sentence is a passive construction. Though spoken, it is a planned piece of informative text, not a spontaneous reminder; the same wording would be re-used again and again in an unvaried intonation. It is also one-way communication.

3 A genuine question (interrogative sentence) from an individual to whom you can reply. The sentence, an active construction this time, is grammatically complete and perfectly well-formed; it is also polite in its use of 'sir'.

4 Again a question to which you can respond, but this time not a grammatically complete one as the subject and part of the verb are missing: '(Have you) got a ticket?' You know it is a question not by its structure but by its intonation. It lacks obvious politeness as you are not explicitly referred to; the focus is back on the ticket.

5 And finally, a case of more extreme **ellipsis** in that rather more words are missing from a notionally complete version: '(Have you got a) ticket, mate?' Again, you recognise it as a question from the way it is said, but now it is over-familiar in its use of slang ('mate') rather than polite. Some people might take offence.

This classification of features allows us to discriminate quite finely between various levels of formality. Each of these five levels, in order of decreasing formality, is identified by its own name:

1 *Frozen* – normally reserved for written language of a highly impersonal and formal nature.
2 *Deliberative* – represents language that has been carefully considered and planned before use. It often includes words from the reading vocabulary.
3 *Consultative* – reflects the sort of language generally used with strangers or persons of only slight acquaintance; it is also the language of general business.
4 *Casual* – a more relaxed style adopted in friendly surroundings.
5 *Intimate* – so called because it incorporates forms and vocabulary normally used only between people who know one another extremely well, such as family, lovers or close friends.

ACTIVITY 26

In pairs compose five sentences, one at each level of formality, with essentially the same meaning. Examples would be requesting silence, asking people not to get out of their seats, or inviting people for a meal. It is important that you imagine a real situation in which the language would actually be used; the situation need not be the same for each level.

COMMENTARY

Register then is concerned with speakers choosing language that is appropriate to the situation they find themselves in. This appropriateness is called **communicative competence**: the speaker's ability to produce utterances that are appropriate and acceptable in context rather than sentences that are merely correct grammatically. Or in simpler language, saying the right thing in the right place at the right time.

Imagine someone in a far-off country learning to speak English as a foreign language. He studies his text books, masters the grammar and a wide vocabulary, reads a variety of English literature, and acquires a Received Pronunciation accent from careful attention to tapes and the BBC's World Service. His English is perfect. Finally, as student of the year, he wins a coveted trip to England! No sooner arrived at Heathrow than he taxis to the East End of London to practise his language skills with the natives. He walks into the first pub he sees and says to the barman, 'Good afternoon, landlord. May I have one pint of your finest bitter, if you please?' Laughs and splutters are heard around the bar, while the barman himself appears worryingly hostile. Meanwhile, a regular customer in need of a refill shouts out, 'Pint er bitta, guv!' That's communicative competence.

Observations on spoken language

Some features of speech that you should have noted about the speaker from the extract on p 26 are:

- Use of 'er' as a **filler** to signal that he is thinking and has not finished speaking.
- Occurrence of pauses of varying lengths.
- Contraction of words so that parts of them are not pronounced: for example, 'you're', 'it's', 'gotta'. Such loss of sound but without loss of meaning is called **elision**.
- Repetition of words or phrases, for example: 'not not', 'you get you get', 'you go up the hill'.
- Self-corrections, for example: 'sign for signs for', 'get into get back into'.
- False starts, where the speaker changes his mind about what he wants to say next: 'you need to it's pretty busy there', 'an' you oh you gotta be'.
- Words or phrases used to check or monitor that the listener is following what is being said, for example: 'OK?', 'right?'. The question mark indicates that the words are spoken with a rising or questioning intonation that helps maintain the interaction.
- Words or phrases used to signal or 'mark' the assumption that both speaker and listener share understanding of what has just been said, for example: 'you know'. These are sometimes called **markers of sympathetic circularity**.
- Use of slang, such as 'bill' for 'police'.
- Regular use of a 'speaking vocabulary' (see Chapter 2) that is basic, short and simple: eg 'need', 'get', 'got', 'want', 'see'.
- Use of vague language that causes something to seem less certain or rather general, for example: 'I think', 'kinda careful', 'gun thing'. These are called **hedges**.
- Use of words or phrases commonly heard in fairly informal speech but

generally avoided in writing, for example: 'OK', 'pretty', 'the old'. These are called **colloquialisms**.

- The omission of words that would normally be included in the composition of a grammatically complete sentence 'I almost got (caught)' but which do not prevent the meaning being clear. **Ellipsis** is the term for loss of words without loss of meaning.
- Exclamation: 'don't get caught!'.
- Use of **speech markers**, words that show the structure of speech by breaking it up into separate chunks. These make clear the sequence of thought in terms of stages, topic switches, asides, summaries, etc, for example: 'so', 'well', 'anyway'.
- Unexpected and brief changes of topic: 'I almost got er'.
- Ungrammatical constructions – 'there's speed restrictions' – where you would write 'there are' not 'there is'.
- Questions. Notice that the question marks indicate the rising intonation of the voice, showing that a question is intended. The actual words spoken are in the form of a statement: 'you 'member' rather than 'do you remember'.
- Frequency of words and phrases referring generally to people, places and times, for example: 'you', 'I' and 'we', 'that' and 'it', 'there'. These are examples of what are called **deictics**, expressions which depend for their meaning on the context, the actual time and place, in which they are used. They point to or 'indicate' the relative positions of the speaker and listener and their shared knowledge. For example 'that pub by the cemetery where we met that time' refers to the particular speaker and listener 'we', who both know the pub in question and recall the time in the past when they met. It would have meant little to anyone overhearing the conversation, and means nothing at all to you reading it now.
- The language is overall loosely connected and lacking in fluency, and this is emphasised by the relative lack of punctuation.

Some reasons for these features in speech are:

- Speech is usually an unselfconscious and spontaneous activity; it is not planned in advance.
- Speech is fast (about 150 words a minute on average) while silences in conversation make people feel uncomfortable; it is simpler and also socially more acceptable to correct or modify what is said immediately rather than spend time planning in advance.
- Speech is harder to remember, hence the frequent repetition of information.
- Speech is what is called context-sensitive. It relies upon shared knowledge in any particular situation, and it makes great use of non-verbal behaviour, especially gesture, facial expression and eye-contact. Hence the use of deictics as a form of verbal shorthand.
- Speech does not need to rely solely on words for conveying meaning. The voice is a highly sensitive and sophisticated instrument for expressing emotions and attitudes by means of such features as stress, pitch, volume, tempo, and intonation.
- Immediate feedback is obtained by the speaker: you see and hear a

response to what you say. You can then alter, adapt, explain, repeat as necessary.

You have learnt about the differences between speech and writing and how some writers incorporate speech features into their writing. You have seen how speakers and writers can foreground language features in order to influence audiences and how they choose language appropriate to the circumstances they are in.

Further reading:

The Five Clocks by Martin Joos. Harcourt Brace Jovanovich (1961). An easy and entertaining exploration of levels of formality.

Patterns of Spoken English by Gerald Knowles. Longman (1987). An extremely useful and wide-ranging introduction to the interplay of speech and writing.

Persuading People by Robert and Susan Cockcroft. Macmillan (1992). A close look at the ways language is used to influence and manipulate people; it will provide useful insights for the whole subject of text analysis.

4 As a Matter of Faction

In Chapter 2 you examined some forms of non-fiction publication, in particular the genre of the textbook, and discovered that the presentation of simple truths and fact was not so simple. In this chapter, using the skills of analysis that you are acquiring, you will look at a range of texts that are a little more problematic. Though they have a foundation in fact, they also incorporate, more deliberately, varying degrees of fiction.

Fact and fiction

You could say that the fiction is created out of the fact, but really the interweaving of the two is often more complicated and subtle. Texts are not easy to unravel, and the emphasis on fact or fiction is by no means always certain.

Faction is the term used to describe texts woven out of fact and fiction in ways that superficially seem to make the separate strands clear. It is a vague term because the boundaries of this genre are difficult to find, but on the other hand it does act as a warning not to take everything on trust! Autobiography, biography, personal memoir and travelogue are examples. On TV the so-called dramadoc, the documentary that reconstructs or dramatises 'real' events using actors, is a prime example of faction.

However, before you examine some examples, it will be helpful to review and summarise what you have learned to date.

Review

You have been focusing on the concept of register by using a set of questions that make up a framework for analysis. This framework allows you to explore a text and discover how it has been woven together to influence its target audience. These questions are varied, showing that register is actually a fairly broad concept, and so it is convenient to subdivide it into smaller areas of inquiry. You can then investigate each of these areas by choosing from a suitably smaller set of questions.

Register is subdivided into three parts. Firstly it includes the topic and purpose of a text, essentially the 'what?' and the 'why?'. Jointly these make up the register's **field**. (You will see the connection with semantic field here.) Relevant questions in the framework of analysis are:

- What is it about?
- When do you think it was written?
- Where exactly would you expect to find it?
- What form or conventions does it display?
- What other texts does it remind you of?
- Why was it written?
- Are the writer's intentions stated openly?

Secondly, register includes a consideration of the participants: the writer and the reader, or the 'who?', and the relationship between them. This aspect is referred to as the **tenor**. As soon as you begin to speak or write, you are creating a relationship of some sort with another person. Relevant questions here are:

- What are the writer's values and background?
- Does the writer use 'I' or 'we'?
- What tone of voice is used?
- What kind of audience is being addressed?
- How can you tell?
- How is the audience addressed or referred to?
- Would you include yourself in the audience?

In examining tenor it is useful to consider the level of formality, as discussed in Chapter 3, as well as the tone (friendly, authoritative, pompous, patronising, serious, humorous, etc).

And thirdly there is the use of language itself, the 'how?'. This is the register's **mode**, and relevant questions here are:

- How is language being used to discuss this topic?
- What mediums are involved in its construction?
- Does it contain characteristics of spoken or written language?
- Does it employ any significant visual features?

You don't necessarily have to ask all of these questions about every text; use only those that are relevant. In most cases the answers to just a few will tell you what you need to know. Remember, you are gathering only evidence that is relevant to a fuller understanding of a text and its effects. You may, by the way, have noticed that the above questions generally speak of 'writer' and 'written', despite the fact that you have already considered a number of spoken texts in this book. While many of the questions do apply equally to speech, this book is concerned not with spontaneous but with prepared examples, involving a degree of scripting.

A definition of register as 'a variety of language appropriate for a specific social use' should now be straightforward. As a speaker or as a writer you have to make choices about the language you use. These choices are affected or restricted by the topic, the purpose, and the people involved in the particular social situation. By asking the framework questions, and using the evidence contained in the separate components of language (phonology, graphology, grammar and lexis), you can arrive at a deeper and more critical understanding of a text. Then you are in a position to evaluate the text by saying what it means to you. This evaluation will often form the conclusion of a written analysis. You are finally answering questions such as:

- How effective ultimately is this text?
- How do I interpret it?
- Am I part of the target audience?
- How do I personally respond to it?
- Do I share its values?

The following text is an extract from *Walking in Central Peakland* by Peter Fooks.

TEXT 25

Rejoining the main track to North Lees Hall, we pass through a gate and join the main farm track, skirting around the nearside of the buildings and descending to the road a little to the west of Cattis Side Farm. Turn right here and follow the road for a little way. Soon after passing a little house ('Brontë Cottage'), a green track will be seen on the left leading to Brookfield Manor, and the footpath to Hathersage follows this track as far as the Manor Gates. At the gates bear left and continue along a path to the left of the buildings before crossing a field to join a track coming down from Cow Close Farm. From here it is plain sailing all the way, for the track leads us unerringly into the centre of Hathersage. We keep to the left of the Hood Brook and, after crossing several fields, the track veers slightly to the right to pass a house, before continuing onward to join a walled lane (Baulk Lane).

ACTIVITY 27

1 In pairs, use the framework for analysis questions to identify clearly the features of the above text. (Note that you don't need to ask all of the questions to complete this exercise.) Summarise in note form the field, tenor and mode of the text, with examples as evidence.

2 In groups, or as a class, compare your assessments and discuss any differences of opinion that may have arisen.

COMMENTARY

You should not have found it too hard to arrive at an agreed analysis for this text. In terms of understanding it's obviously not very demanding, but it does give some useful clues to the way writers create particular types of cohesion, depending on their purpose. Your notes from the activity will contain these clues, though they may need some reorganisation and interpretation.

Grammar

- The six sentences show a mixture of declarative and imperative.
- The tense is mainly present: 'pass', 'join', 'follows', (exception: 'will be seen').
- The voice is mainly active (exception again: 'will be seen').
- Use of deictics includes the pronouns 'we' and 'us' and the adverb 'here'. Notice that the meaning of the pronoun is different for every reader, as it serves to link the writer as a guide to the individual taking the walk. It links the text with a person outside it. On each occasion the adverb 'here' refers within the text to a place just previously described; it also serves to link that place with the physical location of the walker.

Lexis

■ The sentences contain a high concentration of words and phrases connected with walking, and specific landmarks. You could divide them into separate semantic fields:

walking: 'Rejoining', 'pass', 'join', 'skirting around', 'descending', 'Turn right', etc.

landmarks 'North Lees Hall', 'a gate', 'the buildings', 'Cattis Side Farm', etc.

■ In addition, a number of words could be included in both semantic fields: eg, 'main track', 'main farm track', 'the road'. These neatly link the two fields, making the text highly cohesive. **Cohesion** can be defined as 'the way in which words within a text are connected to each other to form a unified sequence'. There are multiple connections in this text, both within each sentence and between them, and they reflect the writer's purpose in providing a clear, detailed and unambiguous set of instructions.

The following three texts are taken from a variety of guide books. The suggested activities, which aim to consolidate and develop analytical skills, follow the third text.

The first comes from an American guide to Disneyworld in Florida, and describes a visit to the 'Expo Center', part of a theme park owned by Universal Studios.

TEXT 26

Back to the Future ***** This flight-simulator-style ride is a super symphony of speed, fantasy, terror and mind-blowing special effects. When it's over, your throat aches because you've unwittingly screamed so long and hard. It's the kind of ride where 12-year-olds do high-fives at the end, then turn to Mom and announce: 'We're going again!'

Based on the *Back to the Future* smash-hit trilogy, the four-minute journey hurls you through centuries at supersonic speed. The action begins in a briefing room where bug-eyed scientist Doc Brown tells guests that Biff (the movie's bully) has come back from the past. As a 'time-travel volunteer,' you must find him and send him back to 1955. Biff dares you, his big-oaf face filling a video screen and taunting:'What are you looking at, butt head!' Eight riders then climb into a fancy DeLorean Time Machine, which spews liquid-nitrogen fog that looks like ice on fire. Your car eerily floats out of its garage, and suddenly you're enveloped by a room-size video screen that takes you on a brain-blasting visual trip: You tumble down waterfalls, soar off cliffs, ricochet around caverns and canyons, and get chomped and spit out by a growling Tyrannosaurus Rex. In the meantime, you're getting bounced around the car and desperately trying to focus on the person next to you.

What Universal did here was take the state-of-the-art simulators used in Disney's Star Tours and Body Wars – and turn up the juice. The sounds, feelings and visuals are all more intense, almost like a fourth dimension. Much of this 4-D realism is created with a 70mm film that's projected on seven-story 'hemispherical' screens around each DeLorean. The ride's electrifying soundtrack comes from a 'multichannel surround-sound' system, and the DeLorean's perfectly timed jolts are fueled by hydraulics. The Back to the Future building itself – a crazy criss-cross of orange, aqua and mustard-color metal – is a real piece of work.

The second text is an extract from *The Blue Guide to Ireland*, describing part of a journey between the towns of Bantry and Tralee.

TEXT 27

Passing (left) the demesne of Ardnagashel, veer north west, skirting **Glengarriff Harbour** (views), backed by the Caha Mountains. In the bay lies **GARNISH ISLAND** (or **Illnacullin**; OPW; 15 hectares), accessible by boat, with its beautiful gardens with their tropical plants, landscaped in 1910–13 by Harold Peto for the then owner, Annan Bryce. G.B. Shaw visited the place in 1923, and here wrote part of *Saint Joan*. The boatmen will practically hurl themselves under your car touting for business, as you enter the village.

Pass (left) Glengarriff Castle before entering the village. **Glengarriff** has a particularly mild climate (mean annual temperature 11°C), making it a pleasant winter resort. Arbutus, fuchsia, yew and holly luxuriate here, their foliage extending down to the water's edge, and the sea, warmed by the Gulf Stream, affords excellent bathing, boating and fishing. At the back of Glengarriff is the 'rough glen' (*Gleann Garbh*) where trees and shrubs fill the crevices between the tumbled glaciated boulders; above rise the bare summits of the Caha Mountains, the graceful Sugarloaf prominent to the west.

Just beyond the village on the left is **Cromwell's Bridge**, a half-ruined structure built, it is said, by order of Cromwell at an hour's notice. Exploration of the numerous creeks, further on, off the Castletownbere road, makes a pleasant excursion. The best of the nearer climbs are **Cobduff** (east; 376m), reached from the Bantry road, and the **Sugarloaf** (west; 574m), reached either from the coast road at Furkeal Bridge or by a track on the north side of Shrone Hill. To the north of the Sugarloaf, between it and the Glengarriff river, is a wilderness of tiny lakes (alleged as usual to be 365 in number), and the larger BARLEY LAKE.

> The third text is an extract from *Wainwright's Coast To Coast Walk*, an account by the famous walker and writer of his 190 mile journey from the west coast of Cumbria to the east coast of Yorkshire.

TEXT 28

From the forest road near Gillerthwaite, the break in the plantations is ascended to the open fellside above the tree-line, the path being unremittingly steep with no features of interest in the immediate vicinity but affording aerial views of Ennerdale and a greater appreciation of the towering bulk of Pillar on the other side, its long summit escarpment and the famous Pillar Rock now being seen in better perspective.

The path scores a bullseye by arriving precisely at the top cairn of Red Pike, and the tedium of the long climb is immediately forgotten as a view of exquisite beauty suddenly unfolds, the ground collapsing dramatically to reveal the Buttermere valley far below and range after range of lofty mountains beyond: a superb prospect.

The ridge to be followed is now seen curving around the cliffs of Bleaberry Comb and rising to the next summit, High Stile, with Pillar still towering above the great gulf of Ennerdale and between them a glimpse of the Scafell group, the highest ground in England.

This is the greatest moment of the walk thus far and a prelude to one of the most attractive high-level traverses in the district. Two hours of thrilling and exciting situations are ahead with the camera working overtime.

ACTIVITY 28

1 In pairs, examine and compare the registers of Texts 27 and 28. (Notice the cohesive effect of the graphology in the case of the former.) In particular, identify the similarities that allow you to place both texts in the sub-genre of 'guide book', as well as the differences that mark out the specific purpose and target audience of each.

2 Then, in small groups, discuss the difference between the texts in their use of descriptive lexis. Compare your findings with the complete absence of emotive lexis in Text 25. Why do these differences exist?

3 Nominate a member of your group to write down an agreed detailed profile for each target audience. Then in large groups or as a class discuss the way in which each text reflects the cultural values and beliefs of its audience: the things that each believes valuable or important to experience. What connection would you make with the selection and presentation of facts in the North American Indian text (Text 14 on page 15)?

ACTIVITY 30

As a class, discuss the relative degree of fact and fiction in the texts you have examined so far in this chapter. What happens to the texts when the fictional element is removed?

A point of view

Facts by themselves are not very interesting or meaningful. You would not read Text 25 simply for the information it contains! Facts generally need some dressing up or colour. The text in which they appear can be woven in a number of ways by the writer, but these ways will be influenced by the writer's purpose and audience. Ultimately, the text must be acceptable to its target audience. They must recognise and accept the register and style, the format and conventions, as being of use or relevance to them. This notion of **acceptability** is crucial to the success of a text; a writer who fails to take this aspect into account is likely to be unsuccessful.

ACTIVITY 31

In small groups, briefly discuss and summarise the key features of language use in Text 25 that make it acceptable to its target audience.

COMMENTARY

Much of the dressing up or colouring involves an invitation, implied or explicit, to share a point of view with the writer. The use of emotive adjectives is one method (see, for example, Text 28). Another is by the use of personal pronouns. You have already seen that a writer's choice of personal pronoun in referring to themselves or to the reader very much affects the tenor of the text, causing it to seem friendly and inclusive or authoritative and distant. In addition, if the writer chooses to refer to themselves as 'I', it is possible to create for the reader the illusion of seeing something through the writer's eyes, so that you appear to see what they see, think what they think and experience everything that they experience. This can be a powerful means of persuading a reader to agree with the writer.

Just before you examine the next text, a brief explanation of how pronoun use is classified. Conventionally, it is referred to in the following way:

- First Person   I (singular), We (plural)
- Second Person   You (singular or plural, depending on context)
- Third Person   He, She, It (singular), They (plural)

The use of the pronoun 'one' is more complex but less common; it almost always introduces a degree of seriousness or formality.

Here then is an extract from *The Lost Continent*, by the American author Bill Bryson, in which he describes his visit to the town of Warm Springs. He is writing in the first person singular.

TEXT 29

In the event, Warm Springs was a nice place. There was just a main street, with an old hotel on one side and row of shops on the other, but they had been restored as expensive boutiques and gift shops for visitors from Atlanta. It was all patently artificial – there was even outdoor Muzak, if you can stand it – but I quite liked it.

I drove out to the Little White House, about two miles outside town. The parking lot was almost empty, except for an old bus from which a load of senior citizens were disembarking. The bus was from the Calvary Baptist Church in some place like Firecracker, Georgia, or Bareassed, Alabama. The old people were noisy and excited, like schoolchildren, and pushed in front of me at the ticket booth, little realising that I wouldn't hesitate to give an old person a shove, especially a Baptist. But I just smiled benignly and stood back, comforted by the thought that soon they would be dead.

I bought my ticket and quickly overtook the old people on the slope up to the Roosevelt compound. The path led through woods of tall pine trees that seemed to go up and up forever and sealed out the sunlight so effectively that the ground at their bases was bare, as if it had just been swept. The path was lined with large rocks from each state. Every governor had evidently been asked to contribute some hunk of native stone and here they were, lined up like a guard of honour. It's not often you see an idea that stupid brought to fruition. Many had been cut in the shape of the state, then buffed to a glossy finish and engraved. But others, clearly not catching the spirit of the enterprise, were just featureless hunks with a terse little plaque saying 'Delaware. Granite'. Iowa's contribution was, as expected, carefully middling. The stone had been cut to the shape of the state, but by someone who had clearly never attempted such a thing before. I imagine he had impulsively put in the lowest bid and was surprised to get the contract. At least the state had found a rock to send. I had half feared it might be a clump of dirt.

ACTIVITY 32

1 In small groups discuss the effect of the writer's choice of first person. To what extent is the text fact or fiction? Decide whether you would include the text as an example of the guide book sub-genre. On what basis did you make your decision?

2 As a class compare your answers to the above questions and reach agreement on the primary purpose of the text.

COMMENTARY

Bryson's book is an example of a travelogue, an account of a personal journey that the reader is not expected to undertake himself. In such texts the writer will recount to the reader what they experienced and how they reacted (though their reasons for doing so can vary). You may have noticed that the particular extract above has many similarities with the story telling genre, for instance in the chronological ordering of events and the regular personal comments of the author. When a writer chooses first person narrative, they appear to share a viewpoint with the reader rather than merely to tell what happened.

By contrast here is an extract from another travelogue, *At Home and Abroad* by V S Pritchett, in which he describes his stay in the Brazilian port of Salvador. Again it is in the form of a first person narrative.

TEXT 30

Salvador is a town of churches and old doorways, of gramophone shops that blare out sambas and tangos all day while the crowd hangs round the doorways listening. The population is chiefly Negro or mulatto. It is a place of cotton frocks, beauty parlors, barbershops. White trousers, white shirts, white frocks, everywhere, give these places a littered appearance. In the superb blue and steaming bay, the steep-prowed fishing boats in the Portuguese style come in with their lateen sails; and the purple pineapples, the bananas, the mangoes and the innumerable other fruits are heaped in the market and carried in baskets on yokes in the street. We never, in the north, eat pineapples like these, without acid or stringiness, as soft as scented water ices to the mouth. The Brazilian picks out his mango and smells it first, as if he were pausing to accept or reject the bouquet of a wine, making sure it has just the right, faint exhalation of the curious turpentinelike fragrance. In tropical countries, the scents and savors of the fruits are a refined pleasure of the senses. They are like wines in their vintages; indeed the fruit of South America is really the wine of the country, and the juices offered at the stalls belong to a world of natural soft drinks that is closed to palates hardened by alcohol. For myself, though I cannot drink the sweet Guarana which is consumed all over Brazil, I find the dry Guarana sold in the Amazon delicious. Most of the whiskey in South America, by the way, is a swindle, the gin deserves only to be drowned, the lager beer is excellent and the various vodkalike fire waters are for desperation.

ACTIVITY 33

1 **a** In small groups compare Texts 29 and 30, initially by using the framework for analysis. What contrasts do you detect in the level of formality and tone? Do these contrasts reflect any difference in the purposes of each text?
  b You may have noticed that Bryson's attitude to events is very negative, while Pritchett's is correspondingly positive. How are these attitudes communicated to the reader?

3 As a class, discuss the particular features of either Bryson's or Pritchett's register that make up his individual 'stylistic fingerprints'.

4 Then, on your own, rewrite one of the texts in the style of the other. Conclude with a paragraph in which you identify the features of the style that you have adopted, and comment on any difficulty you experienced in carrying out the exercise.

4 Choose a place that you know well and write a short description of it:
  a for inclusion in a guide book
  b for inclusion in a travelogue.

NOTE: A further activity for Text 30 is provided in Chapter 5 (page 52).

(Auto)biography

You might well conclude that a significant distinction between biography and autobiography will lie in the writer's choice of pronoun. It should not therefore be surprising that many biographies of living celebrities are 'ghost written' by someone else and presented as autobiographies in the first person. A writer using first person narrative appears to share information and a viewpoint with the reader; the reader in turn may then unconsciously adopt the position of the writer and accept uncritically what he reads. In this way the writer is often said to 'position the reader', and this process of positioning will be referred to again in the chapter on advertising. A writer choosing to use third person narrative often appears far more objective; the reader is less aware of some particular person's view. Of course, both forms of writing can be persuasive in their different ways.

A comparison

The following two texts are accounts of the first meeting between Diana, Princess of Wales and Prince Charles. Andrew Morton's revised biography, based largely on tapes recorded for him by the Princess, included edited extracts from them. As part of the 'raw data' for his work, you might consider them a sort of unpolished autobiography. The first extract is from a tape (any words in brackets are not the words of the Princess); the second extract is Morton's reworking of this material.

TEXT 31

I've known her [the Queen] since I was tiny so it was no big deal. No interest in Andrew and Edward – never thought about Andrew. I kept thinking, 'Look at the life they have, how awful' so remember him coming to Althorp to stay, my husband, and the first impact was 'God, what a sad man.' He came with his labrador. My sister was all over him like a bad rash and I thought, 'God, he must really hate that.' I kept out of the way. I remember being a fat, podgy, no make-up, unsmart lady but I made a lot of noise and he liked that and he came up to me after dinner and we had a big dance and said: 'Will you show me the gallery?' and I was just about to show him the gallery and my sister Sarah comes up and tells me to push off and I said 'At least, let me tell you where the switches are to the gallery because you won't know where they are,' and I disappeared. And he was charm himself and when I stood next to him the next day, a 16-year old, for someone like that to show you any attention – I was just so sort of amazed. 'Why would anyone like him be interested in me?' and it *was* interest. That was it for about two years. Saw him off and on with Sarah and Sarah got frightfully excited about the whole, then she saw something different happening which I hadn't twigged on to, ie when he had his 30th birthday dance I was asked too.

TEXT 32

It was during her sister's romance that Diana first came into the path of the man considered then to be the world's most eligible bachelor. That historic meeting in November 1977 was hardly auspicious. Diana, on weekend leave from West Heath School, was introduced to the Prince in the middle of a ploughed field near Nobottle Wood on the Althorp estate during a day's shooting. The Prince, who brought along his faithful labrador, Sandringham Harvey, is considered to be one of the finest shots in the country so he was more intent on sport than small talk on that bleak afternoon. Diana cut a nondescript figure in her checked shirt, her sister's anorak, cords and wellington boots. She kept in the background, realizing that she had only been brought along to make up numbers. It was very much her sister's show and Sarah was perhaps being rather mischievous when she said later that she 'played Cupid' between her kid sister and the Prince.

If Charles's first memories of Diana on that fateful weekend are of 'a very jolly and amusing and attractive 16-year-old – full of fun', then it was no thanks to her elder sister. As far as Sarah was concerned Charles was her domain at that time and trespassers were not welcomed by the sparky redhead who applied her competitive instincts to the men in her life. In any case Diana was not overly impressed by Sarah's royal boyfriend. 'What a sad man,' she remembered thinking. The Spencers held a dance that weekend in his honour and it was noticeable that Sarah was enthusiastic in her attentions. Diana later told friends: 'I kept out of the way. I remember being a fat, podgy, no make-up, unsmart lady but I made a lot of noise and he liked that.'

ACTIVITY 34

1 Read both texts carefully. In pairs draw up a list of the differences in terms of content, tenor, mode, and any other features you think relevant.

2 Then in small groups discuss how these differences are related to the use of first or third person narrative. Is there any difference in the primary purpose of each text?

3 In pairs, one of you should rewrite Text 31 in the third person and one rewrite Text 32 in the first person. For example, Text 31 might begin 'Diana had known the Queen since she was tiny ...', and Text 32 'It was during my sister's romance that I first came into the path of the man ...'.

4 Compare your attempts and assess how realistic they are. What difficulties or problems did you encounter and how successful do you think you were in overcoming them?

5 In groups or as a class review the common difficulties encountered in the previous activity. How do you think these difficulties restrict or broaden a writer's opportunity to express themselves freely?

Review

This chapter began by introducing the idea that some classes of text include elements of both fact and fiction. You should now be in a better position not only to identify these separate strands but also to assess whether the particular 'mix' in a text is justifiable in terms of audience and purpose. This chapter has also highlighted an area where the world of fiction can be seen most obviously to influence the world of fact. Hence the term faction, a meeting ground for both where the boundaries are sometimes obscure. This is an opportune moment to introduce the notion of **intertextuality**.

Intertextuality

Intertextuality is a very useful term for discussing the relationship 'between' (Latin 'inter') texts. You don't read a text in isolation. When you read any text you bring to it your accumulated experience of reading a number of similar texts. You relate the text, usually unconsciously, to others of a similar type. This is how you recognise a text as a flyer, a receipt, a recipe, a guide book, etc. In addition, you will have certain expectations about the content, style and appearance of a text based on this personal database.

Often the links between texts are strong. Look at any recipe book, for example, and you will find that the only difference between the individual recipes is in the ingredients, not in the style and format of the language. The recipes display a high degree of intertextuality. However, the comparison of two recipes in Chapter 1 demonstrated that significant differences can occur within even the same sub-genre. There the degree of intertextuality was strong enough for you to recognise both as recipes, but you were also aware of the differences.

Your reading of any text, then, relies upon your knowledge of other texts, whether similar (from the same genre or sub-genre) or dissimilar (from a different genre or sub-genre). Writers often deliberately link their texts to other types for effect – a sort of 'pick-n-mix' – and these links can often stretch across from one genre to another. As you have seen in this chapter, writers often rely upon your knowledge of forms of fiction when they are providing you with facts. The idea of intertextuality will be discussed further in later chapters.

ACTIVITY 35

In groups discuss the idea that writers of guide books and travelogues need to include aspects of fictional writing in order to make their texts acceptable to their target audiences. You should perform this activity by close reference to the texts discussed in this chapter or to relevant texts of your own choosing. In either case some days' preparation is advisable to ensure a productive debate.

A final text follows that will be helpful in developing the skills of analysis explained in this chapter. It is the opening paragraph of Peter Ackroyd's biography of the poet and artist William Blake.

TEXT 33

In the visionary imagination of William Blake there is no birth and no death, no beginning and no end, only the perpetual pilgrimage within time towards eternity. But we cannot follow him into that bright world, not yet, and his story must begin above a hosier's shop in Soho where, at 7.45 on a November evening in 1757, he came crying into the rushlight and candlelight of a London winter. We may be able to see, if we look hard enough, the doctor's lantern and the fire of sea-coal that greet the piping infant; but the outlines of those who attended the birth remain shrouded in the deepest obscurity. Blake was later to invoke the 'Angel at my birth' and 'The Angel that presided o'er my birth', but he remained strangely silent about his own more immediate family. The little that is known about them can be related here, as the infant is bound tightly in swaddling clothes before being returned to his mother.

ACTIVITY 36

1 In pairs or small groups identify the elements of fact, fiction and opinion in the text. What is the effect of Ackroyd's occasional use of first person plural narrative? What happens if you change it to first person singular? Or third person?

2 In large groups or as a class discuss how effective you think the opening is. Provide reasons based on your analysis of the language used.

3 On your own find two further examples of biographical beginnings that you believe contrast in their use of language. Write a brief description of each and explain their essential differences.

You have seen how writers can incorporate elements of fiction into their non-fiction texts and have been introduced to intertextuality, the relationship between texts.

Further reading:

Language and Literature by George Keith. Hodder & Stoughton (1999). A wide-ranging introduction to the various genres encountered in the world of fiction, for those who wish to pursue the links discussed in this chapter.

Grammar, Structure and Style by Shirley Russell. OUP (1993). Contains a basic description of register as well as explanations of many other fundamental aspects of language relevant to the analysis of texts.

Language, Ideology and Point of View by Paul Simpson. Routledge (1993). Includes two very helpful chapters on point of view as applied to non-literary texts.

5 It's Official!

In this chapter, and using the framework for analysis as a starting point, you will examine the ways in which language is used for official purposes within society. You will develop your skills of analysis, particularly in discovering devices for cohesion in texts and in the effects possible through a writer's choice of lexis. You should then have a greater understanding of the difficulties that writers face in making texts acceptable to a target audience.

We will look at some varieties of language used in official circles: the law and government, bureaucracy, business, and educational institutions. We can examine only a few examples here, but as in the other chapters of this book, you should try to find further examples of your own so that you can practise the skills of analysis that you are acquiring.

Legal language

The legal system is one of a number of traditional institutions that are fundamental to the society we live in. As such it has its own distinct variety of language that many people outside the profession perceive as long-winded, pompous, dull and largely incomprehensible. Yet lawyers claim that it aims always to be absolutely clear and unambiguous. How can such opposing views be reconciled, if at all? To begin with, here is an extract from a piece of legislation central to modern life, and that members of the legal profession would refer to in their everyday work: Section 4 of the Road Traffic Act 1988, as amended by the Road Traffic Act 1991.

TEXT 34

4 Driving, or being in charge, when under influence of drink or drugs

(1) A person who, when driving or attempting to drive a mechanically propelled vehicle on a road or other public place, is unfit to drive through drink or drugs is guilty of an offence.

(2) Without prejudice to subsection (1) above, a person who, when in charge of a mechanically propelled vehicle which is on a road or other public place, is unfit to drive through drink or drugs is guilty of an offence.

(3) For the purposes of subsection (2) above, a person shall be deemed not to have been in charge of a mechanically propelled vehicle if he proves that at the material time the circumstances were such that there was no likelihood of his driving it so long as he remained unfit to drive through drink or drugs.

(4) The court may, in determining whether there was such a likelihood as is mentioned in subsection (3) above, disregard any injury to him and any damage to the vehicle.

(5) For the purposes of this section, a person shall be taken to be unfit to drive if his ability to drive properly is for the time being impaired.

(6) A constable may arrest a person without warrant if he has reasonable cause to suspect that that person is or has been committing an offence under this section.

(7) For the purpose of arresting a person under the power conferred by subsection (6) above, a constable may enter (if need be by force) any place where that person is or where the constable, with reasonable cause, suspects him to be.

(8) Subsection (7) above does not extend to Scotland, and nothing in that subsection affects any rule of law in Scotland concerning the right of a constable to enter any premises for any purpose.

> *The Highway Code*, published by The Stationery Office, includes a summary of important law affecting road users. Its summary of the whole of Text 34 follows:

TEXT 35

Drinking and driving
You **MUST NOT**:
• drive under the influence of drink or drugs.

> A rather startling difference! What could be clearer, you might think, than the version in *The Highway Code*?

ACTIVITY 37

1 a In small groups, analyse Text 34. In particular, establish the key aspects of mode, tenor and purpose, with appropriate textual evidence for each. Nominate a person from each group to summarise your findings.

  b Who specifically is the target audience? Draw up as detailed a profile as possible. Why is the language of the text acceptable to them?

2 In larger groups or as a class compare and discuss your findings.

3 What significant features of Text 35 make it appropriate and acceptable to its target audience? Why is this text unsuitable as a piece of legislation?

When you have completed this activity, you should read the relevant commentary at the end of this chapter. You will need to be aware of the comments before you read on.

ACTIVITY 38

1 In groups of two or three, choose in turn one sentence from Text 34 and rewrite it in a style suitable for a textbook aimed at GCSE law students. You may need to use more than one sentence for some sections.

2 As a class assess the relative success of your rewrite, and discuss why your version is unsuitable as a piece of legislation. What difficulties did you find in accomplishing the exercise?

ACTIVITY 39

1 Imagine you are writing a guide for young people who have just passed their driving test. In small groups write a suitable paragraph explaining the relevant parts of Text 34.

2 Compare your versions. How did you decide what content to omit? What register have you adopted and why is it suitable?

Part of the explanation for the difficulty and monotony of Text 34 lies in the complete absence of a personal voice or expression of emotion. It is woven in shades of grey rather than bright colours, but this is the way it has to be in order to fulfil its purpose. This restricted way of using language highlights something else about a writer's choice of vocabulary and about the meaning of words. You can find the meaning of any word in a dictionary. After all a dictionary is a work of reference: the ultimate authority for writers and readers, to say nothing of the many competitions, crosswords and media shows (*Call My Bluff*, *Countdown*, etc) that rely upon it. But a dictionary provides only part of the story.

Take the word 'baby', as defined in three current dictionaries:

- 'an infant, young child' (*Chambers Twentieth Century*)
- 'a newborn or recently born child; infant' (*Collins English*)
- 'An infant of either sex' (*Shorter Oxford*).

You wouldn't disagree with these, but you might think them rather basic and limited. They provide just the 'core' meaning, relating the word to the outside world. It is the real and literal meaning, it is objective and value-free, it is unemotional. And that of course is all that 'baby' means when it is used in a leaflet on immunisation or in a manufacturer's instructions on bottle feeding.

What does the word 'baby' mean to you? In everyday life it is likely to remind you of young families, love and affection, innocence, pink and blue outfits, care and comfort, dependence, helplessness, vulnerability, cuteness, the mystery of renewal, potential for growth, cooing, crying, dirty nappies, and so on. These represent important aspects of the word 'baby', but they are not generally found in a dictionary. They are additional associated meanings that show people's emotions and attitudes. There seem, therefore, to be two kinds of meaning here, and they are distinguished by separate terms. The basic literal meaning is the **denotation**; the extra associations constitute the **connotations**. Some connotations of words are particularly emotive, that is, they can arouse strong emotions in the reader. The use of words for their denotations rather than connotations characterises Text 34, and helps explain its impersonal nature.

ACTIVITY 40

1 **a** In small groups examine the following words: *flowers, cat, blood, champagne, jeans*. Nominate one person to write out your agreed denotation for each (the definition you might expect to find in a dictionary).
b Write down as many connotations for each as you can think of.

2 As a class compare your results. Review your total range of connotations for each word. To what extent do these depend upon a person's age, background or culture? How are the connotations affected by the context in which a word appears?

ACTIVITY 41

1 a In groups select three of the following words from Text 34: *person, vehicle, drink, drugs, constable, premises*. Write down as many synonyms as you can. Under 'constable', for example, you might start with 'cop', 'pig', 'bobby', 'filth'.

b Then organise the words into lists that share similar connotations. Do these separate lists suggest certain types of text for their use?

2 If you have previously carried out Activity 10 in Chapter 2 (p 18) in which you developed a semantic field from a core word, discuss how your understanding of the term semantic field has been expanded.

ACTIVITY 42

Turn back to Text 25. Discuss in what way is it similar to Text 34.

ACTIVITY 43

1 Turn to Text 30 in Chapter 4 (page 44). The semantic field of fruit is obviously important here. Nominate one person to write out all the words and phrases that fall within this field. What connotations do they have? What other semantic fields are referred to and how do their connotations contribute to the total effect?

2 To what extent would a shopping list containing pineapples, bananas, mangoes, wine, and soft drinks have a different effect? What factors would account for the difference?

Warning!

The next two texts are the opening sections of publications by commercial organisations selling products: Microsoft for Windows 95 and W H Smith *Do It All* for dimmer switches. The main purpose of each is to warn the customer about aspects of using the product, but you should be able to recognise and explain the differences between them.

TEXT 36

End-User License Agreement For Microsoft Software
MICROSOFT® WINDOWS® 95

IMPORTANT – READ CAREFULLY:This End-User License Agreement ('EULA') is a legal agreement between you (either an individual or a single entity) and the manufacturer ('PC Manufacturer') of the computer system ('COMPUTER') with which you acquired the Microsoft software product(s) identified above ('SOFT-WARE PRODUCT' or 'SOFTWARE'). If the SOFTWARE PRODUCT is not accompanied by a new computer system, you may not use or copy the SOFTWARE PRODUCT. The SOFTWARE PRODUCT includes computer software, the associated media, any printed materials, and any 'online' or electronic documentation. By installing, copying or otherwise using the SOFTWARE PRODUCT, you agree to be bound by the terms of this EULA. If you do not agree to the terms of this EULA, PC Manufacturer and Microsoft are unwilling to license the SOFT-WARE PRODUCT to you. In such event, you may not use or copy the SOFTWARE PRODUCT, and you should promptly contact PC Manufacturer for instructions on return of the unused product(s) for a refund.

TEXT 37

WH SMITH DO IT ALL
ROTARY DIMMER SWITCHES
(SINGLE OR DOUBLE DIMMERS FOR REPLACING
SINGLE OR DOUBLE SWITCHES ON ONE WAY
LIGHTING CIRCUITS)

General Notes:

■ Use only on an electricity supply of 200–250 volts 50 cycles per second.
■ Do not use with fluorescent lamps.
■ The dimmerswitch may be fitted to a wall box having 60.3mm screw fixing centres and a minimum depth of 16mm (ie a normal plaster depth flush box, or a normal surface mounted switch box). It must **not** be fitted into a metal box having 4 fixing lugs. If such a box is already fitted into the wall, the top and bottom lugs **must** be broken off.
■ Dimmerswitches having a metal front plate must be earthed by means of the earthing point provided on the dimmer.
■ Dimmers must not be overloaded or underloaded. Maximum 400 watts, minimum 60 watts, total lighting. 2 Gang (double) Dimmers have a maximum capacity of 500 watts of lighting (250 watts per side – minimum 60 watts per side).
■ A slight buzzing may be heard from the dimmerswitch in operation. This is quite normal.
■ Read instructions below carefully. Incorrect installation may damage the dimmer beyond repair. In case of any doubt or difficulty consult a qualified electrician.

ACTIVITY 44

1 **a** In pairs, identify the main characteristics of the register of each text. You should find several similarities, so what features distinguish them from each other?
 b In particular, look at the lexis. There are semantic fields of computing and electrical fittings in Texts 36 and 37 respectively, representing the jargon of the computer user and the electrician. However, Text 36 also contains other jargon and a format (ie, graphology and grammatical structure) that indicates a specific key purpose. What is this purpose and who exactly is included in the total target audience?

2 What other purposes, apart from warning, is Text 37 intended to serve? What problems faced the writer of this text? Did he solve them successfully? (In other words, did he make the text acceptable to the target audience?) Be sure to provide textual evidence in support of your answer.

3 Next turn back to Texts 4 and 7 in Chapter 1. In groups:
 a agree upon the primary and secondary purposes of each text
 b identify their similarities and differences. Nominate one person to write down your agreed reasons for the differences in register between the four warnings that you have now examined.

ACTIVITY 45

In groups, look again at Texts 34 and 36. Both share a legal semantic field – how would you separate them in terms of audience and purpose? What textual evidence can you provide?

ACTIVITY 46

1 As a class, discuss what types of warnings occur in society and where they are displayed.

   a Then, on your own, collect at least six examples of warnings. Write a brief introduction to the nature and importance of intertextuality. Remind yourself of the discussion on intertextuality on p 47. Show how the concept applies to your examples.

   b Write an analysis of two texts from those you have collected, explaining the similarities and differences between them.

The following text is an extract from another government publication: *A Buyer's Guide* issued by the Office of Fair Trading for the general consumer. In this section a number of legal phrases (in italics) are discussed.

TEXT 38

BUYING A SERVICE

When you pay for a service – for example, from a dry cleaner, travel agent, car repairer, hairdresser or builder – you are entitled to certain standards.

A service should be carried out:

with reasonable care and skill – a job should be done to a proper standard of workmanship. If you get a new extension to your house, the walls should not start to crack and the roof must not leak;

within a reasonable time – a garage should not take weeks and weeks to repair your car. You can always agree upon a definite completion time with the supplier of the service;

at a reasonable charge, if no price has been fixed in advance – if the price was fixed at the outset, or some other way of working out the charge was agreed, you cannot complain later that it is unreasonable. Always ask a trader how much a particular job will cost. The trader may only be able to make an informed guess at the cost and give you an estimate. If you agree a fixed cost it is usually called a quotation. A fixed price is binding whatever it is called.

Where materials (such as bricks or wallpaper) are used in the provision of a service, or it involves fitting goods (such as double-glazing or radiators), the materials and goods are covered by the law in the same way as when you buy them directly.

Whether you are buying goods or services, it could be worth checking, before you part with your money, whether the business or person providing the service is a member of a trade association. Membership does not guarantee satisfactory work, but if anything goes wrong, it could make it easier to get things put right.

ACTIVITY 47

1 On your own, briefly identify the main aspects of the text's register: its field, mode and tenor.

2 In small groups:

   a reach agreement on the register of Text 38, in particular its purposes.

   b To what extent do you think the text achieves its aim of being user-friendly for its target audience?

   c In what way does it differ from a text book?

ACTIVITY 48

Collect as many examples as possible of texts containing words used solely or mainly for their denotations. After a week, bring these texts to a group discussion and classify them into types or genres. Are there any significant or recurring types of text?

Here are two texts sharing some similarities of purpose but presented in highly contrasting ways. Text 39 is the front of a form that can be used by travellers on London Underground to claim a refund in certain circumstances; Text 40 is a standard letter of apology sent to passengers who complained about local rail service provision by Wales & West during early 1999.

TEXT 39

Our Customer Charter

Our commitment

London Underground aims to deliver the best possible service for all its customers. You want a quick, frequent and reliable train service, a safe, clean and welcoming station environment with up-to-date information and help-ful, courteous staff. This means a continuous, demanding programme of improvements to meet rising expectations.

Our targets

To drive and measure these improvements, performance targets covering many aspects of our service have been agreed with Government as part of the Citizen's Charter programme. If you would like to know more, please contact our Customer Service Centre, which is open between 0830 and 1730, Mondays to Fridays, on 0171–918–4040. We regularly publish our performance against the targets. Train service performance infor-mation is posted at every station and details of other targets are available from the ticket office.

Our refund pledge

If you are delayed more than 15 minutes because of our failure, we will give you a refund voucher to the value of the delayed journey. Please claim by filling in this form. We cannot give refunds in circumstances which prevent us from safely running trains such as a security alert, freak weather or because of action by a third party; nor when we have publicised in advance an alternative route, for example because of planned engineering works. Special conditions apply if we have an industrial dispute. Extra claim forms are available from any station or the Customer Service Centre.

Your feedback

If you have any complaints or suggestions on how we can improve our service, please contact your local manager. The address and telephone number are displayed in the ticket hall.

CITIZEN'S CHARTER
Improving Service
UNDERGROUND

TEXT 40

Dear Mr Dean

Thank you for contacting us regarding the difficulties you experienced during your recent journey. We would like to apologise for the time it has taken to respond to your letter and for not delivering the high quality service our passengers expect.

Wales & West has recently experienced a period of unsatisfactory performance both of our train services and related net-work problems. We are investing heavily to improve the quality and reliability of our trains, the availability of accurate and timely information, and the level of service provided by our staff. We are also working with other train operators, suppliers and Railtrack to drive through improvements to the rail network and infrastructure to make them more reliable and user friendly.

Due to the amount of correspondence recently received by us, we regret that we are unable to answer your specific points, however, all your comments have been registered within our customer database and will be forwarded to our company directors on a regular basis.

Already we have as a result of customer feedback introduced a no smoking policy throughout our fleet of trains, we are currently investing over £1.5 million into totally refurbishing our Class 158 trains. We are committed to providing in-formation systems at all stations within our franchise agreement.

We apologise for the disruption caused to your recent journey and as per our Passengers Charter, we have enclosed travel vouchers to the value of £13 which we hope you will use towards a future rail journey. These vouchers are valid for 12 months and are accepted by all Train Operating Companies.

Yours sincerely

Catrin L Evans

Catrin Evans
External Affairs Assistant

You should now have the confidence to analyse both texts in order to establish the characteristics of their registers. The following activity therefore concentrates on details of the texts.

ACTIVITY 49

1 On your own, and in advance of the following activities, you should analyse each text. Write in note form a summary of its register in terms of field, mode and tenor.
2 In small groups compare and reach agreement on your analyses. Both texts use lexis to promote a positive image, yet both also contain lexis with negative connotations, particularly Text 40. Why is this negative language used, and what is the effect in each case?
3 Discuss:
   a What particular effects are achieved by the differing formats of charter (Text 39) and letter (Text 40)?
   b More specifically, how does the choice of format affect the choice of pronoun adopted by the writer to refer to the organisation and the customer? What is the intended effect in each case on the target audience?
   c Do your answers confirm your earlier assessment of the purpose and tenor of each text, or do you need to modify your original evaluation?

Parody

If you compare two similar texts you are likely to notice aspects of each one that that you might not have observed if you had looked at only one text.

Read the following pair of texts: Text 41 is part of the foreword to a booklet giving instructions on the installation of a Pentium computer's mainboard; Text 42 is the opening of an article by Bill Bryson in *Night & Day*, the supplement to The 'Mail on Sunday'.

TEXT 41

Foreword

Thank you for purchasing the AB-PX5/AX5/TX5 as the heart of your computer's system. We hope this instruction booklet will enable you to install PX5/AX5/TX5 in your system safely and without any errors. Although you may be familiar with some of the concepts we will explain, please read over them again to avoid any problems.

1 The motherboard in most PCs use many connecting cables to connect peripherals to the main unit. The important thing to remember is that these cables all have a 'direction'. Later in the chapter, we will talk more about the definition of connecting cables and the method of installation. Please pay special attention to our prompts. Because we are using the exclusive ABIT SOFTMENU™ technology to modify the motherboard, the jumper is not required

anymore. We also use simple and easy to understand software design to complete the task. Because of this, you can install the motherboard directly into the system. However, we still suggest you first carry out a simple test before you install the motherboard inside the computer.

2 In this booklet, we will write out in full any new technical words we encounter for the first time and use their contractions thereafter.

3 If, when you are installing the CPU problems occur and there is no way to solve them, we suggest you first clear the CMOS information (refer to Chapter 2). If you still have problems, contact us.

4 How to perform a simple basic test? It's simple. Place the motherboard on a flat insulated surface (like the packaging the motherboard came in). Plug the CPU into the ZIF socket (if you are installing a fan, install it on top). Plug DRAM module in and then plug the keyboard in. Plug in the electrical cord (ensure electrical supply is turned **off** when doing this) and pay attention to polarity (refer to Chapter 2). Plug in the display card and plug the 15 Pin D-Sub monitor signal connector into the display card. Make sure the connections are correct and secure and then turn on the power source for the monitor and then the main power supply. If a picture appears on the monitor, congratulations, the basic test has been successful. Finally, good luck with the complete installation.

TEXT 42

Congratulations. You have purchased an Anthrax/2000 Multimedia 615X Personal Computer with Digital Doo-Dah Enhancer. It will give years of faithful service, if you ever get it up and running. Also included with your PC is a bonus pack of pre-installed software – Lawn Mowing Planner, Mr Arty-Farty, Blank Screen Saver, and East Africa Route Finder – which will provide hours of pointless diversion while using up most of your computer's spare memory. So turn the page and let's get started!

Getting ready: Congratulations. You have successfully turned the page and are ready to proceed. (Important meaningless note: the Anthrax /2000 is configured to use 80386, 214J10 or higher processors running at 2,472 herz on variable speed spin cycle. Check your electrical installations and insurance policies before proceeding. Do not tumble dry.) To prevent internal heat build-up, select a cool dry environment for your computer. The bottom shelf of a refrigerator is ideal.

Unpack the box and examine its contents. (Warning: Do not open box if contents are missing or faulty as this will invalidate your warranty. Return all missing contents in their original packaging with a note explaining where they have gone and a replacement will be dispatched to you within 12 working months.)

The contents of this box should include some of the following: monitor with mysterious De Gauss button; keyboard with 2 inches of flex; computer unit; miscellaneous wires and cables not necessarily designed for this model; 2,000-page *Owner's Manual*; *Short Guide to the Owner's Manual*; *Quick Guide to the Short Guide to the Owner's Manual*; *Laminated Super-Kwik Set-Up Guide for People Who Are Exceptionally Impatient or Stupid*; 1,167 pages of warranties, vouchers, notices in Spanish, and other loose pieces of paper; 292 cubic feet of styrofoam packing material.

Something They Didn't Tell You In The Shop: Because of the additional power needs of the pre-installed bonus software, you will need an Anthrax/2000 auxiliary software pack, a 50-megahertz oscillator unit for the memory capacitor, 2,500 mega-gigabytes of additional memory for the oscillator, and an electrical sub-station.

Setting Up: Congratulations. You are ready to set up. If you have not yet acquired a degree in electrical engineering, now is the time to do so.

ACTIVITY 50

1 In small groups, discuss the register of each text. What features do they share in terms of lexis and grammar? Do you detect any difference in the use of jargon? Nominate one person to write agreed lists of:
   a the shared features
   b the differences between the texts. What is the key difference?

2 As a larger group or class compare your findings. What aspects of register are crucially different in the two texts? Would you include yourself in either target audience?

When you have completed these activities, you should read the observations that appear at the end of this chapter.

Review

In this chapter you have examined a number of texts published by various official bodies. One area that you have concentrated upon is lexis: the distinction between denotation and connotation, the use or avoidance of jargon and its cohesive effect, and the way in which vocabulary from a number of semantic fields can be interwoven for particular purposes and effects. You have also examined some important differences in the way such texts select information for numerous purposes: to explain, warn, record, advise, assist, reassure, persuade, convert, encourage, instruct, promote a viewpoint, or argue a case. In fact, information is rarely used simply to inform!

Many official texts share several linguistic characteristics. You have certain expectations about their appearance and use of language, and so you recognise them when you come across them. This recognition is the basis of intertextuality, which allows writers to make links between texts and readers to perceive them. However, you cannot predict every aspect of a text. Texts 39 and 40 included similar content but were drafted in contrasting formats. There is no reason why Text 39 shouldn't be in the form of a letter, and Text 40 a charter. Writers generally have options available at some level of graphology, lexis, formality, grammar or format, except where tradition or convention have 'frozen' a text into a specific and extreme form (for example, legislation). The best writers choose the options best suited to their purposes.

With this idea of options in mind, we will now examine a number of texts sharing the same purpose and published by similar institutions. University prospectuses for undergraduates include some form of introduction to the prospective student. Here is The University of Sheffield prospectus (1999 edition):

TEXT 43

Welcome from the Vice-Chancellor, Professor Sir Gareth Roberts

Welcome to the University of Sheffield's Prospectus for undergraduate students. We hope you will find it interesting and informative and assist you in making those very important decisions about where and what to study.

With nearly a century of achievements in top quality teaching and research, the University of Sheffield retains its position as one of the UK's leading higher education institutions. This has been confirmed in recent independent quality assessments where both teaching and research have been highly rated. With over 60 departments and 900 academic staff, the University offers a wide range of courses and the modular course structure provides flexibility and choice.

Student life is not solely concerned with academic pursuits and Sheffield provides plenty of entertainment and leisure activity. Students are able to enjoy the University's own Sports Centre and Drama Studio, the facilities of one of the best Students' Unions in the country, and all the facilities of a large city.

We are confident that if you choose Sheffield you will become one of our many happy and successful students. If you have any queries please do not hesitate to get in touch, or, better still, discover the University of Sheffield for yourself on one of our Visit Days.

COMMENTARY   As you would expect, this introduction is consistently positive and confident in outlook. Its content is clearly marked by its paragraph structure: first, a general welcome that identifies the institution and target audience; second, a promotion of the institution; third, student lifestyle; fourth, general assurances and invitation to open days. Overall, the topic is clearly the attractions of being an undergraduate at Sheffield, the purpose to convince prospective students that they should seriously consider applying. But a closer scrutiny of this text is more revealing. Although it is but one page out of 260, it is fair to assume that the Vice-Chancellor accurately reflects the attitude of the University to its students. Here are just a few observations.

The use of pronouns is not entirely consistent throughout the text. The Vice-Chancellor uses 'we' in the first paragraph, and 'we' and 'our' in the fourth: three occasions in all. Typically a person of status or responsibility who can officially represent an organisation or institution uses 'we' and 'our'. It is a convention that allows this person to, as it were, officially speak for that organisation or its effective members. It can often be somewhat vague in reference, but it can also make the message seem more personal. In contrast here, the middle paragraphs avoid this usage, though it would have been possible to write for instance: 'With nearly a century of achievements in top quality teaching and research, *we* retain *our* position as one of . . .'.

Why did the writer not choose this option? Part of the answer may lie in the opening of the last paragraph: 'We are confident that if you choose Sheffield'. The reference to Sheffield is ambiguous – is it the city, the university, or both? Whichever it is, the 'we' is kept separate. It appears that the institution, with its prestigious reputation gained over nearly a century, is deliberately distinguished by the writer from the current staff, who can represent only a tiny proportion of those who have contributed to its present status. The text tries to give an impression of a respected place of learning on the one hand, and of a dedicated staff on the other. Does it succeed? Well, three instances of the first person plural are perhaps too few to ensure the establishment of a sufficiently personal tone. Some opportunities to reinforce this personal aspect were not taken; for instance the last sentence might have read: '. . . do not hesitate to get in touch *with us*'. Of course, the reader is addressed as 'you', but again this occurs only in the first and fourth paragraphs.

There is also little evidence of spoken language in the text. True, 'get in touch' is rather colloquial, while 'better still' is certainly informal, but otherwise the lexis and sentence structures are firmly those of the written language. The level of formality varies. The central paragraphs are deliberative, the first and last consultative (the evidence lies largely in the pronoun usage). Likewise the tone is impersonal in the central paragraphs, though it is positive, authoritative, and assured throughout.

You should have no difficulty in discovering how a positive image is promoted in the text. The choice of lexis, the use of declarative sentences containing a large number of facts and figures, and the choice of tense all contribute. It would also be well worth identifying the semantic fields that occur and the proportion of nouns and adjectives that are polysyllabic and of French or Latin origin. All of which might lead you to refine the purpose and target audience.

For The University of Sheffield, the prospective student is not just any student, but a particular type of student: the type who will maintain the traditions of the institution by an appropriate attitude to the academic and social life available. The purpose of the text is to indicate the sort of student who should apply and, by implication, to dissuade a less desirable sort from even considering an application. The target audience is not 'students', but more specifically students possessing certain desirable qualities. The Vice-Chancellor, in seeming to welcome readers, is also making an ideological statement about the place of the University in society and its membership. But if this is true, will the target audience recognise it? The point was made in Chapter 1 that the key question for a writer is not 'What do I want to say?' but 'How do I want to influence the reader?'. Do you think the readers will recognise the writer's (slightly idealised) intentions? Will they reconsider whether they are included in the target audience?

The above observations are meant to stimulate further analysis; they are by no means complete or comprehensive. You have been developing skills of observation and description, but by themselves these aren't enough. So, for instance, you might notice the use of 'we' and 'our', identify them as a personal pronoun and related possessive adjective, and even count their frequency. But this is only the first stage in analysis. You must use the information you have gathered in order to comment, explain and evaluate the text. As a language specialist you are examining the text to criticise it, to assess its strengths and weaknesses, and discuss its effect.

The writing of an introduction to a university prospectus is difficult, and is subject to regular revision. Sheffield's 1998 version was somewhat longer, the main difference being an extra paragraph that followed the first:

Choosing a university is not easy: you will need to consider courses, accommodation, location, sporting and cultural facilities, and – although it may seem far away – your future after graduation. Sheffield has a great deal to offer its students both in terms of academic opportunities and life in a large, lively and friendly city.

ACTIVITY 51

In small groups, in the light of the previous observations, consider the extra paragraph in the 1998 Sheffield prospectus. Do you think its inclusion in the 1999 edition would affect the tenor of the text? Give reasons for your response. Would you re-instate the paragraph or not? Why?

The following texts are introductions to the Universities of Stirling and of Lancaster.

TEXT 44

Welcome from the Principal and Vice-Chancellor

A Miller

I joined the University of Stirling in 1994 having worked in five other universities. There is no doubt that Stirling is different and offers many real attractions as a place to study. This prospectus should help you see at a glance if Stirling is the place for you.

What is distinctive about Stirling? First, it is a young university built in 1967 on a superbly beautiful campus sited in an eighteenth century estate, linked by a short bus ride to the Royal Burgh of Stirling. I am still impressed that the calm setting in which we work is nevertheless close to a thriving town and the two main cities of Scotland, as well as to the Scottish Highlands.

The campus experience is special. The size of the University means that it is possible for us to get to know each other personally. Accommodation is available for all first-year students who want it, and the campus also offers top level sports facilities and a wide range of social facilities, including the MacRobert Arts Centre, and the Students' Association's Robbins' Centre.

Stirling has a reputation for student-centred teaching methods rather than subject or teacher-centred approaches. It was the first UK university to divide the academic year into two semesters rather than three terms, and to develop modular course structures which allow ready credit transfer. Stirling also replaced assessment based wholly on examinations by a unique blend of periodic testing and examination. The selection of courses on offer is designed to allow students to keep their options open for as long as possible and to permit maximum choice of subject combinations.

I do hope that as you read through the prospectus you will see that Stirling is a university where you could fulfil your ambitions both personally and academically and equip yourself for the future. Some of Stirling's advantages such as the superb campus could be just luck; having one of the lowest student drop-out rates in Scotland, however, is not just luck. Please try to visit the campus and see for yourself; after all, I would say it's great, wouldn't I? Whatever you decide, I wish you all the best for your future.

Professor A MILLER MA BSc PhD FRSE
Principal and Vice-Chancellor

TEXT 45

Welcome to Lancaster University

Choosing a university at which to spend the next few years of your life is not easy. As a student, you will be making a financial as well as a personal commitment to your future. It is important to make sure that you choose the right course at the university that best suits your needs. There are many questions that you will want answering on a variety of different topics which is why we try to provide as much information as we can through our Prospectus, university web site, and departmental booklets. We hold numerous departmental open days throughout the year so you can have a look around the campus and talk to our staff and students directly. We also have an extensive Alumni network, national and international, which can put you in touch with former students who can provide friendly and practical advice about Lancaster University.

Make use of the contact points provided in this Prospectus – we are here to help you decide if Lancaster University is the place for you. If it is, then we will match your commitment.

William Ritchie

Professor William Ritchie
Vice-Chancellor

ACTIVITY 52

1 In groups, compare Texts 44 and 45 with Text 43 (on p 58). Make separate notes of their similarities and differences, but remember that any 'missing' information is likely to be found elsewhere in the relevant prospectus.

2 Discuss the way in which each writer has portrayed the institution and addressed the

target audience. Is the selection of
information in each case the most suitable
for purpose and audience? To what extent
would prospective students find each text
acceptable?

3 In the light of your discussion, do you think
the writers have in mind any readers other
than prospective students? How might this
affect the style of writing?

4 There are about 100 UK universities
publishing prospectuses annually. Find three

or four further examples that display
variations in their approach and use of
language. Write an analysis of these,
focusing on their acceptability to the target
audience.

5 Choose one introduction which you feel you
could improve and, using any other
information in the prospectus you think
useful, rewrite the text.

6 In small groups, test out your rewritten
version for feedback on its effect.

ACTIVITY 53

1 Re-read the section that discusses genres in
Chapter 2 (pp 23–24). Look again at the
texts you have studied in the present chapter
together with any other similar texts you
have found for yourself.

2 Then consider the following questions:
   a Are official publications a genre?
   b Can they be divided into a number of
   identifiable sub-genres?

c Or are the potential differences or options
so great that they fall into more than one
genre?
   d How **do** you classify them?

3 When you have prepared written answers in
note form to the above questions, in large
groups or as a class debate your views.

COMMENTARY
On Text 34

You should have had little trouble in establishing the main features of register found in the Road Traffic Act from an examination of the text's
graphology, grammar and lexis. In terms of mode the text contains no aspects of spoken language whatsoever. This helps explain why in terms of
tenor the level of formality is frozen, the tone impersonal, authoritative and
serious. The purpose of the text is not just to inform citizens of the relevant
law, but to form a permanent record for posterity and act as the ultimate
reference in cases of dispute.

The text exhibits some characteristics that are common in the legal register
and worth noting.

Graphology

■ The section is divided into clearly visible subsections by numbering,
paragraphing and spacing – a way of visually 'chunking' the information.
■ There is very little punctuation, given the length and complexity of
some sentences.

Grammar

■ Each sentence is structured so that it is independent of the others. It is a
self-contained unit of meaning, and this is reinforced by the graphology.
The links within each sentence create a rather odd structure, as what
might be more naturally expressed in two or three sentences is
compressed into only one. For example, the way in which the first

sentence is built up can be appreciated by simply pulling it apart, working from the outside in. At the end the basic simple sentence would be 'A person is guilty of an offence'. An extra piece of information is then inserted to identify the type of person ('who is unfit to drive through drink or drugs'), and another piece is inserted within that to explain the relevant time ('when driving or attempting to drive a mechanically propelled vehicle on a road or other public place'). One piece of information is therefore 'embedded' within another. Sentence two works in much the same way. Each sentence aims to express its meaning clearly by providing the reader with everything he needs to know in a logical sequence. At every twist and turn of the sentence the writer must prevent any possible misinterpretation by the reader.

- Links between sentences are explicit. Each sentence is itself also a subsection and is referred to by its number.
- Ellipsis is not used. For instance, you might expect sentence two to read 'such a vehicle' instead of repeating 'a mechanically propelled ... public place', or to end 'is also guilty', because the vehicle details and the offence have been mentioned in sentence one. But this would prevent the sentence remaining self-contained.

Lexis

- The semantic field of the law is evident in technical words like 'guilty', 'offence', 'court', 'constable', 'warrant', 'arresting'. It also includes a more formal and specific lexis, such as 'deemed', 'determining', 'conferred', and certain phrases that regularly occur to express legal concepts ('Without prejudice', 'reasonable cause') or to link pieces of information in a consistent way ('For the purposes of').
- There is regular repetition of lexis, already explained in the comments on grammar above.

Though the language may seem cumbersome, convoluted and stilted, it is a necessary evil for the legal profession. The graphology, grammar and lexis are here quite intricately interwoven to form a unique pattern, one which makes very clear the types of cohesion used. However you react to it, there is no doubt that this language has been most carefully composed.

Such a short extract can display only a selection of the features that make up the legal register. And in any case there are further finer distinctions between the language of statutes, of legal forms (such as contracts and wills), of briefs, of correspondence, of courtroom procedure, and so on. As with any occupation or profession, the various situations will be reflected in the stylistic differences of the register. However, they will all share a common core, or store, of lexis. This lexis, then, comprises the shared words and phrases necessary for the practice or understanding of a particular occupation or topic. It is a collection of technical terms (the terminology) often referred to as **jargon**, the understanding of which separates the practitioner or specialist from the man in the street.

COMMENTARY

On Texts 41 and 42

In Text 42 Bryson imitates many of the features of the Pentium text. You should have identified clearly the jargon which is common to both, and the additional invented 'jargon' that Bryson introduces for humorous effect.

You should also have had little difficulty in distinguishing the separate purposes and tenor of each. Bryson has here written a **parody** of a computer user manual. A parody not only copies certain stylistic features of a text, it also highlights or exaggerates them in clever and imaginative ways. The writer foregrounds selected features with the intention of being amusing, of being satirical, of poking fun at anyone or anything pretentious or pompous. Despite its surface humour however, a parody often works at a deeper level, introducing a note of seriousness and criticism.

Naturally, then, for parody to work you have to recognise it. In other words you must be acquainted with the type of text that is being imitated. The notion of intertextuality helps explain how parody works. You notice both the similarities and the crucial differences, as well as the contrasts in purpose and tenor.

ACTIVITY 54

1 Find an official text issued by an organisation or institution. Analyse its register and identify the particular characteristics that make it recognisable – its 'stylistic fingerprints'.
2 Choose a couple of representative paragraphs from the text and, in the light of your analysis, write a parody of them.
3 As a subsequent group or class exercise, exchange these parodies for members to identify the type of text on which they are based.

In this chapter you have learnt about:

- the importance of lexical cohesion within texts
- the difference between denotation and connotation
- the effect a writer's choice of words can have on the target audience
- the variety of purposes served by informative texts.

Further reading:

Words and Their Meaning by Howard Jackson. Longman (1988). A sound introduction to types of meaning and the effect of word choice.

6 An Explosion Of Magazines. . .

In this chapter you will examine both general and more specialist magazines in order to develop an understanding of audience needs and the way in which writers and publishers satisfy them. You will review types of text, such as horoscopes and letters, that recur in a variety of magazines, in order to uncover audience differences. And you will develop your skills of analysing the writer's attitude to both audience and topic.

Walk into any large newsagent and you will find several hundred magazines catering for a wide range of age-groups and interests – and these are only a selection of the most popular. In addition, many magazines are available by subscription to organisations, or are supplied free of charge by commercial bodies.

Earlier in its history, the word 'magazine' meant a general-purpose storehouse, and a little later more specifically a place where arms and gunpowder were kept secure. In 1731 *The Gentleman's Magazine* appeared, described in its introduction as 'a monthly collection to treasure up, as in a magazine,' information on a wide range of subjects. The shelves have been exploding regularly ever since. To begin with, here is the first half of an article from a magazine.

TEXT 46

Black Magic

John McKenna on the mysterious properties and enduring popularity of coffee

Let us be perfectly unambiguous about coffee. The cup that rests in your hand as you read this, the cup that sits beside my computer as I write this, is there for precisely the reasons outlined by Claudia Roden in her book about the magical bean.

'Few beverages are as intoxicating, heartwarming and utterly satisfying as a steaming cup of freshly made coffee,' she writes. 'There is the flavour, the stimulation and the colour, there is body and 'point' (sharpness) and above all there is the aroma'.

Let us not kid ourselves. Ms Roden's language suggests a respectable drink, and isolates its positive factors. But there are a few giveaway adjectives nestling in her delicate sentences, and it is those scrupulously polite plaudits, 'intoxicating' and 'stimulation,' which tell us what coffee is really all about.

It is a drug, possibly the greatest drug of all, and we crave its drug-rich properties.

The proof of this lies in its history. Coffee first became popular in the Middle East – our word coffee derives from the Arabic *qahwah*, a term which etymologists explain as a term for wine – and with the discovery of the drink came the first coffee houses.

With the arrival of the coffee houses came the first attempts to suppress these congenial meeting places on the grounds that not only did the potent new potion excite the drinker, but it also encouraged political subversion.

Muslim scholars sought to prove that coffee was proscribed by the Koran, and edict after edict condemned and closed the coffee houses in Constantinople, Mecca and Cairo.

The award for the most assiduous pursuit of coffee drinkers must go to the Ottoman Grand Vizir Koprili, who not only prohibited coffee, but made cudgelling a punishment for a first offence, and the rather tidy solution of placing second offenders into leather bags which were then sewn up and tossed into the Bosporus.

ACTIVITY 55

Relevant to this text are two closely-linked questions from the framework for analysis: 'Where exactly would you expect to find it?' and 'What kind of audience is being addressed?'

1 In pairs or small groups, analyse the register of this text. In particular, draw up a target audience profile, establish the general tenor of the text, and agree upon its primary purpose.

2 In larger groups or as a class compare and discuss your findings, and then name three magazines in which you think the article might appear.

The observations on the text at the end of this chapter are not intended as a comprehensive analysis, but you should now read them before continuing further.

Regular features – what's in store?

Despite considerable variety in content and target audience, many magazines contain regular features of a similar nature. One of the most common and popular is the horoscope. Here are four star signs from a Christmas edition of *B*, a magazine targeted at females aged 18–25.

TEXT 47

CAPRICORN (DEC 22–JAN 20)

Give yourself a break from the problems of those around you and concentrate on what *you* want. From the 12th you may overspend so make a list before you go shopping and stick to it. If you need to negotiate, wait until after the 21st, when you're more likely to get your own way. **Your personal challenge**: With Mercury in retrograde up until the 27th, make sure you double-check your Christmas arrangements.

TAURUS (APR 21–MAY 21)

A time of change is approaching, so you may feel very up and down. But there is the chance of success, especially if you grasp unexpected opportunities. If you have to deal with figures of authority, get them on your side. You should have the chance to catch up with your chums around Christmas. **Your personal challenge**: While money should be flowing to you as usual, make sure you handle it a little more wisely this month.

LIBRA (SEPT 24–OCT 23)

Early in the month, make the most of your charm to get what you want. From the 12th onwards, with the help of Mars and Venus, there could be more than one romantic surprise . . . Don't worry if your home life seems a bit up and down. By the 22nd everything should fall into place. Watch out for good news around the 29th. **Your personal challenge**: With Mercury in retrograde until the 27th, double-check all important arrangements.

SCORPIO (OCT 24–NOV 22)

The focus will be on work and money until the 10th when minor details will need to be ironed out. When Venus and Mars move into Aquarius, you're likely to be more interested in your home and social life. From the 18th you should get a chance to let your hair down and the 24th will give you the opportunity to win someone over. **Your**

personal challenge: If you want to keep balanced, give yourself a break from your family around the New Moon on the 29th.

1 Obviously, predictions about the future are less than certain. In small groups, find examples in the text of how language is used to convey:
a uncertainty
b certainty.
Though you should examine the sentence types and lexis generally, pay particular attention to the way that verbs are used to indicate activities. Nominate one person to draw up two lists of methods with examples from the texts.

2 In larger groups or as a class compare your findings. How would you describe the tenor of this text? Does the writer's way of addressing the reader affect their response to the horoscopes?

When you have completed this activity, you should read the observations at the end of this chapter. Then read on.

Going! . . . going? . . . not gone

You have been meaning to visit an elderly relative. 'Are you going then?' you are asked. And you think to yourself: 'Yes. I *will* go . . . I must go . . . I should go . . . I can go . . . well, I could go . . . I might go . . . well, I would go . . . No.' Your attitude to going changes from the initial positive, through certainty, insistence, obligation, ability, good possibility, not so likely possibility, and serious doubt, till you reach your final decision.

Most verbs are described as 'main' or 'lexical'. Each expresses its own individual meaning, and each in its basic form, prefixed by 'to', is referred to as the **infinitive**. So: 'to smile', 'to sing', 'to fight'. These work well enough when straightforward facts are reported:

They are fighting; he was fighting; they have been fighting; she had been fighting.

And so on. Whoever was involved and whenever it happened, some fighting has been going on. But sometimes there is doubt, and sometimes absolute certainty, and that's where help is required in the form of a small group of verbs called **modal auxiliaries**. They are auxiliaries because they belong to a class of verbs whose job is to be a help (Latin: 'auxilium') to the lexical verb. Here are the most common ones:

can	may	will	shall	must
could	might	would	should	ought to

These modal auxiliaries are unusual as they possess no infinitive form. There is no verb 'to may', 'to would' or 'to must' (there is a verb 'to can', but only in a factory). They also have no independent status – they depend on lexical verbs for their existence. Modal verbs add something extra to the straightforward meaning: they add what is called **modality**. In other words, they add the attitude of the speaker or writer to whatever he is saying or writing. These attitudes include possibility, probability, uncertainty, intention, necessity, obligation, insistence, ability, definiteness and permission.

ACTIVITY 57

In pairs, take the simple sentence 'Otto and Xena fight', and in turn insert each of the above ten modal verbs ('Otto and Xena can fight', 'may fight', etc). Decide what extra meaning or modality each modal verb expresses.

COMMENTARY

In one sentence you may not always find as many as ten different meanings when you use the ten modal verbs.

Sometimes the context or tone of voice is needed to clarify the meaning. For example, 'Otto and Xena may fight' could be granting them permission or expressing a possibility.

You cannot equate any one modal with any one meaning. For example, 'can' expresses ability in 'Bridget can speak Maltese'; permission in 'Can we go now?'; and possibility in 'Everyone can make a mistake'.

Note that 'will' and 'shall' have uses as modal verbs in addition to their common function of expressing the future.

ACTIVITY 58

On your own, take the ten common modal meanings (possibility, probability, etc), and compose sentences that use as many different modal verbs as possible to communicate each. For example, definiteness/certainty could be expressed by:

Fish <u>will</u> die out of water.
It <u>must</u> be gone six o'clock.
I <u>shall</u> go to the ball.

Of course, modality can be expressed by other means. Adverbs like 'possibly', 'probably', 'perhaps', and 'maybe' will all act as formal hedges, while more colloquial forms such as 'sort of', 'kind of', and 'like that' will do the same in speech. If you look back at Text 47, you will now appreciate how probability and possibility are conveyed not only by the modal verbs, but also by modal phrases like 'more likely', 'a little more wisely', 'likely to be'. But modal verbs are very powerful little words, useful as a sort of verbal shorthand for revealing attitude. They are grammatical rather than lexical, and again demonstrate that grammar can give meaning just as much as choice of vocabulary.

Here is a star sign from 'Style', the magazine supplement of *The Times*:

TEXT 48

LEO

July 22–August 21

As the week commences, you could find yourself so absorbed in battles over unexpected developments or enforced changes that you are not entirely aware of opportunities that could substantially alter elements of your daily life. Some involve your work or obligations, others proposals that are related to your health and wellbeing; whatever their exact nature, the fact that they are indicated by your ruler, the Sun, at odds with the planet of growth and opportunity itself, Jupiter, means what you learn should be worth the trouble in the long run. Issues involving financial matters may not be quite so easily resolved, particularly since they also seem to involve affairs of a creative or romantic nature. This is no occasion to waste time quibbling over details. Since the events that accompany next week's stunning planetary activity will demand your full attention, settling matters now clears the way for fast action.

1 In pairs, list with examples the ways language is used to convey both certainty and uncertainty. How is the language different from that of Text 47? (Pay special attention to the lexis, sentence structure and tenor.)

2 In small groups compare your findings. What purposes do Texts 47 and 48 perform?

How does the different use of language reflect the different target audience?

3 In pairs or on your own, rewrite Text 48 by removing or replacing all language that indicates any uncertainty. Can your version still be classed as a horoscope?

1 In groups of two or three, collect examples of horoscopes from as varied a range of magazines as possible. After a week, bring them in and list their common features. Some aspects, like graphology, will vary considerably. How do these stylistic differences within the register of horoscopes reflect the different audiences?

2 What sort of magazines didn't include a horoscope page? Were you surprised at any of these? How does their omission reflect the target audience profile?

The bunny bug

The notion of audience may seem an easy one to understand, yet often your immediate response to a text, especially if you have some personal opinion or feelings on the topic, is not completely objective. The following text is the first portion of a longer article from a far more specialist publication, the *Shooting Times & Country Magazine*.

TEXT 49

CONEY IN SIGHT

IT TOOK me a little by surprise recently to learn that a couple of friends have been culling rabbits on a regular basis with a .22 air rifle. Yet on the face of it I ought not to have considered it too seriously. For many years as a schoolboy I harvested summer rabbits with an airgun and accepted it as normal practice. In recent years, however, I have talked to many sportsmen who have insisted that airguns do not have the power to make clean kills.

Not having used an airgun (apart from a target pistol) for many years, I assumed that perhaps those earlier old weapons had greater power than those around today. I have no way of knowing and, since my own preference is for a silenced .22 semi-automatic rifle, I thought it doubtful that I would ever put the theory to the test. I confess, nevertheless, that I was very impressed with the results reported by a keeper friend – 17 clean kills out of 20 shots with an air rifle. I did not see it all happen, but there were the carcasses (of many different sizes) to prove the point.

The air rifle, he said, was an old one that had lain neglected in the loft for about 18 years and was only taken out on a whim. He and I had been shooting together with my own weapon for some time, but during my absence abroad he felt the need to carry on the good work. Where rabbits are in plague proportions, all-out war has to be declared.

One of those airguns that needs to be pumped up to pressure succeeded well enough, he told me, but having to 'recharge' the thing between shots was time-consuming and noisy. He was not impressed.

On for a hat trick

Several times we have shot two rabbits sitting together without causing alarm. I have many times taken three myself without moving from my stand. There is nothing very smart about that. A semi-automatic reloads itself for as long as shells remain in the chamber. The bullet travels without sound and as long as target rabbits are not scared, it is only necessary to squeeze the trigger again and again. I was, however, duly impressed to learn that my friend had scored a hat trick with this regular old air rifle.

Having seen him shoot accurately from both shoulders with equal ease, I am fairly certain that little or no luck was involved. Head or neck-shot rabbits seldom manage to kick themselves down holes before they are gathered!

ACTIVITY 61

This main purpose of this text is to provide an experienced sportsman's opinion on a technical aspect of shooting, yet some of the vocabulary used by the writer also betrays his personal attitude both to shooting and to his target audience.

1 On your own, find the words and phrases that display his attitude. Substitute others for these which keep as far as possible only the denotative meaning, so that you convert the text into a purely objective and factual account. (For example, in the first paragraph you could replace 'culling' by 'shooting a number of' or 'picking out', and 'harvested' by 'gathered' or 'shot'.)

2 When you have written them all down, exchange your amendments with those of your neighbour and evaluate their relative success. How is your response to the text altered? What difficulties did you experience in accomplishing this task?

3 In small groups, discuss and write down the writer's assumptions about the shared knowledge and values of his target audience. What is your evidence from the text? (You should examine jargon and the way in which his lexis expresses his attitude.)

Nice and nasty

You will have noticed that the writer, as well as displaying a professional pride in accurate shooting, often expresses a detached view when describing the actual killing. He uses words and phrases that portray shooting as a useful, natural, or painless activity, and that mask the reality that many would find more violent. He speaks of 'culling' rabbits which are 'harvested'; kills which are 'clean' and constitute 'good work'. An activity that many would find cruel and distasteful is made socially inoffensive and acceptable. **Euphemism** is the term for such words and phrases. They make nice what many feel to be nasty.

In many cultures some topics are referred to in polite or indirect ways, at least in most social situations. Excretion, certain illnesses, sex and death, for example, can be quite delicate topics and may need to be discussed with euphemisms, avoiding possible offence. Alternatively, of course, you can easily offend or embarrass people by a less sensitive lexical choice. These **dysphemisms** are socially much nastier! At the extremes, for urinating you have the difference between 'powder my nose' and 'piss', for diarrhoea 'the collywobbles' versus 'the shits', for copulating 'make love' versus 'fuck', and for death 'fell asleep' versus 'rubbed out'. Your choice will depend on the social situation you're in. And that situation will restrict your options, at least for as long as you wish your words to be acceptable to your audience.

Euphemisms and dysphemisms can occur in connection with any topic or group that becomes socially sensitive. Employment, class, age, race, religion and gender are regular candidates, but the list is endless. Though they share denotative meaning, the connotations of euphemisms and dysphemisms are naturally quite different and often highly emotive. They give strong clues to a writer's attitude and purpose. In the war of words between people, dysphemisms are the weapons, euphemisms the shields.

In the bag

One regular feature in numerous magazines is the letter spot. And this needn't be just a problem page. As a recurring item, letters provide a clear insight into the needs and interests of the target audience. Here is a small selection.

TEXT 50

From *TV Hits*

Prodigy to tour!

I'm really into Prodigy and I'd love to go and see them play live, so could you let me know when they're touring and whether they're planning to play in Birmingham or anywhere near?

Prodigy fan, Derby

Well, you've got a while to wait for a full tour because The Prodge aren't going to be touring until November, when they'll be doing a full UK tour which'll include Birmingham. However, if you can't wait that long, you could try catching them at one of the festivals over the summer. It's been confirmed they're headlining the V97 festival at Chelmsford and Leeds on August 16 and 17, alongside Blur, Kula Shaker, Ash and The Bluetones.

TEXT 51

From *Motoring & Leisure*

Mini minus lead

My wife has a 1976 Mini Clubman Countyman Estate 1100cc which we are told will not run on lead-free petrol. It would seem that the Broquet Fuel Catalyst might well be our answer to the problem of the cessation of leaded petrol in the year 2000. Having heard conflicting views as to whether the device works or not, could we hear at first hand from anyone with a similar Mini or other car which now runs happily on lead-free with Broquet. Are the valve seats still in good condition and was any adjustment required to the engine timing?

E Keeling, Dorset

TEXT 52

From *Current Archaeology*

Whitley Grange

The plan of Whitley Grange (CA 157) showed a walled enclosure some 23x32 metres flanked by very substantial bathing facility with a 6 metre square paved room and an adjoining hearth (kitchen?). Combined with this, two sides of the main area had some sort of covered arcading. Since the whole structure was within sight of a major road, could this be the Roman equivalent of a caravanserai?

HENRY MEIN, Rivermere, Main Road, Bleasby, Notts, NG14 7GH

TEXT 53

From *FHM*

In praise of hippies

Who is the tosser who writes the replies to the letters in FHM? Judging by the remarks he made about men with long hair (in reply to M. Proctor's letter, August 1998) he must be bald. I happen to be a married lady who loves long hair. If there is one thing that turns me right off, it's the sight of trendy twats with their nauseating short cuts – particularly when worn with suits or clothes with sports logos. Sad old hippies? Bollocks. And as for M. Proctor, your hair sounds really sexy. Can I have a photo of it to drool over?

Rowena Cunliffe, Merseyside

So, the advantage of having long hair is that strange married women want to gob all over it? No wonder hippies always look so greasy.

ACTIVITY 62

1 In groups, read all four texts. What differences are there in choice of lexis and tenor? What kind of knowledge and values are shared by writer and reader? Draw up a profile for each target audience, using evidence from the texts.

2 Compare your audience profiles with those of other groups. To what extent do the letters give clues away about the typical reader?

3 In groups, write down:
   a why only some letters have a reply
   b what purposes are served by each text
   c to what extent you believe the letters are genuine, rewritten or invented
   d why they have been published as letters rather than some other format (eg diary of events, feature, editorial).

4 Compare and discuss your views with other groups.

Postbag postscript

You are now practised in analysing typical letters from a range of magazines. You have uncovered ways writers choose language that will be acceptable to their target audience. Turn back to Texts 12 and 13 in Chapter 1. The problem in each case is similar but the replies are different in approach, content and tone. *J-17* is aimed at girls of 12–18, *Cosmopolitan* at females in their mid-20s.

ACTIVITY 63

On your own, analyse Texts 12 and 13 carefully, paying special attention to the replies in terms of lexis, modal verbs, and purpose. Write an analysis, including an explanation of how these features differ and why each target audience is responsible for any differences.

ACTIVITY 64

In groups of two or three, collect letters with a common theme from a varied selection of magazines (the agony aunt or uncle column is an clear example, but sports or computer magazines for different audiences will also provide suitable material). After a week, bring them in and list both their shared features and their stylistic differences. How do the latter reflect the specific readers?

ACTIVITY 65

On your own, choose one magazine and summarise its contents in terms of topics and presentation. Then select three extracts (say, a letter, part of an article, editorial, interview, feature, review, etc) and identify the similarities in use of language (type of lexis, graphology, tenor, etc). Write your analysis, showing how closely the writing styles are similar or dissimilar, and explain your findings by describing the audience profile.

Whose voice?

A very common feature in magazines is the interview with the celebrity, the star, or the person currently in the news. Here are the openings of two: an interview from *Kerrang!* with the musician Jerry Cantrell, and from *Shoot* an interview with footballer Keith Gillespie.

TEXT 54
SWAMP THING

'I don't *do* heroin, so you're talking to the wrong guy,' bristles Jerry Cantrell. 'I'm not denying anything and I'm not f**king saying that anything *is* true. I'm just sick of talking about it, so I'm not gonna talk about it any more. There you go!'

Cantrell unleashes one of his alarming machine-gun laughs. Until now, the *Kerrang!* journalist had seemed like a nice bloke. He had gone almost 40 minutes without broaching the subject of heroin addiction – specifically, whether it has contributed to *Alice In Chains'* two-year spell in limbo.

'It just gets *old* talking about it,' sighs the guitarist. 'There's nothing new to say.' On the contrary, Jerry Cantrell and *Alice In Chains* have rarely spoken frankly on the subject of any drug problems they might have, despite the fact that their gruelling 'Dirt' album from 1993 peered so convincingly through the eyes of a junkie.

Cantrell's last comment on the subject was made to *Kerrang!* in October 1992: 'It's public knowledge that Layne (Staley, A/C singer) and I had some (drug) problems. That's way over, that's already been taken care of. The music on 'Dirt' is the final nail in that coffin.'

Cantrell isn't about to give us an update. He will, however, chat enthusiastically about 'Boggy Depot', his naked-ly confessional debut solo album. Doesn't mind talking about his life, either. So we'll stick with that for a while. Then we'll casually ask what the f**k happened to *Alice In Chains*.

The Boggy River cuts through the property Jerry Cantrell's family own in Oklahoma. The nearby state park is called Boggy Depot.

'I wrote a lot of the album parked in a car by the bank of that river, thinking about Oklahoma,' Jerry explains. 'It's a very personal record for me. A big accomplishment, after being in a band for so long. Change is good. You can get a little too comfortable, where you maybe stop growing.

'Not that I ever felt that way in Alice,' he swiftly adds. 'But this was an opportunity to try unfamiliar territory.' Had Cantrell always fancied doing a solo album? 'Probably . . .' he cautiously begins.

TEXT 55
Keith Gillespie

THIS IS GOING TO BE A VERY IMPORTANT SEASON FOR NEWCASTLE, ISN'T IT?
'We had a very disappointing season last time and we're going to have to improve on our league position. Obviously we were delighted with getting to the FA Cup Final but we weren't pleased with our overall form in the League. We had injuries to key players but we'll still be looking for a huge improvement on last year.'

IS THERE A MORE SERIOUS ATTITUDE AROUND THE CLUB THIS SEASON?
'Yeah, we were disappointed for the fans as much as ourselves. Thirteenth place in the League after coming second in the previous two seasons is not really acceptable, so we want to prove to everybody that we can do a lot better than that and we're concentrating hard on doing it. We've got quite a few new signings so hopefully they can come in and do the business and we'll be challenging again this season.'

DO YOU THINK THE FANS EXPECT TOO MUCH SOMETIMES?
'I don't think so. It's hard at times living up to their expectations but we know no matter how things go they'll be behind us. In return for that we've got to provide the club with the honours that they deserve for following us for so many years. They haven't really had too much to cheer over the last 12 months so anything we gain will be a return for their loyalty.'

IS IT IMPORTANT THAT NEWCASTLE WIN A TROPHY THIS YEAR?
'I think it's a necessity that we're up there. I don't think the Newcastle fans will accept a season like last year – that's plain for all to see. They want to see us up there with the best and challenging for trophies. If we don't win anything this season and come second in the Premiership, but have a good Cup run, then I think the fans will be a lot happier than they were at the end of last season. Having said that, of course we want to provide them with a trophy as a reward for their support through thick and thin.'

ACTIVITY 66

1 The contrasting styles of these interviews are both very commonly used in magazines. In groups of two or three, list what you think are the important differences in the way they

are reported. In particular, you should examine the structure of the texts and the role played by each of the interviewers. Provide examples from the texts to support your observations.

2 How accurately do you think each text reproduces the words spoken by the interviewee?

3 Do you prefer one style of reporting to the other? What different effects are achieved by each? Do you think one method is more 'truthful' than the other?

4 In the light of your responses, what do you think are the purposes of each text?

When you have completed this activity, turn to the end of this chapter where you will find some observations on the texts, together with a further activity.

Review

In this chapter you have examined types of text that recur in various forms in many magazines. Your examination of these differences has shown how writers regularly make choices in language, and how these choices match the expectations that their readers have about both content and style. Throughout this book you have examined small texts or parts of texts, but magazines are of course made up of a large number of individual texts. It is a job of the magazine editor to ensure that overall there is sufficient consistency in style throughout the publication, so that it meets the needs and expectations of its readers. Part of this consistency in approach is achieved by the magazine 'house style': the editor's guidelines on both the appearance of the page (fonts, punctuation, colour, illustrations, etc) and the writers' way of expressing themselves. Together these should provide a unique form of cohesion to the publication, making it acceptable and recognisable to its target audience.

You can think of a magazine as a text containing smaller texts: texts within a text. The trick is to make those smaller texts sufficiently varied yet identifiably similar.

COMMENTARY

On Text 46

Your analysis of the text would, among other things, uncover the following:

■ Paragraphs are short, and reflect the small 'chunks' of information or opinion offered by the writer.
■ Content is a varying mixture of fact and opinion: the first and third paragraphs are virtually pure opinion, the seventh appears largely factual, the others fall somewhere in between.
■ Content is also diverse for such a short text: the properties and characteristics of coffee as a drink; its use as a drug; its origins; historical attempts to ban it.
■ The lexis ranges markedly from the speaking vocabulary to the writing (see Chapter 2): from the colloquial 'kid ourselves', 'giveaway' and 'tossed' to the more literary 'plaudits', 'proscribed' and 'assiduous'.
■ At the outset, the writer involves the reader very deliberately by identifying with them: 'Let us be . . .' is followed by a description of the simple shared experience of drinking coffee.

This is a strange text. Despite its detail and its more unusual lexis, it doesn't seem very demanding. In fact, it may very well have struck you as quite ordinary. How has the writer achieved this?

Well, the short paragraphs suggest visually that the content is light and undemanding, a technique widely employed by magazines and newspapers. The variety of information reduces the need for concentrated attention; if you don't quite understand something you can ignore it without losing the thread of the whole piece. It also encourages you to continue reading. The early relationship established between writer and reader is developed and sustained in several ways: by the use of the pronouns 'us' and 'we' in the third and fourth paragraphs; by colloquialisms; by the degree of personal opinion offered and by the flippant manner in which some facts are related: 'The award for the most . . .', 'rather tidy solution'.

You are therefore constantly aware of the writer's 'voice' as you read, a voice that speaks to you as an equal ('we', 'us') in a relaxed, occasionally humorous, and knowledgeable way. And because the tone is obviously not patronising, you accept the polysyllabic and more unusual lexis. In fact, this more literate lexis is deliberately overdone to add to the lack of seriousness; 'scrupulously polite plaudits' and 'potent new potion' are foregrounded for comic effect by their repetition of similar sounds – they sound just too contrived. You have explained what appeared irreconcilable about the extremes of lexical choice.

To summarise, then, the text provides a number of separate facts all associated with a common drink shared by most people in Western culture. It has no specific focus and is clearly personal and informal. Is the purpose to inform, to educate, to enlighten? The text is too unfocused and undemanding for these to be anything but secondary. Information is there, but it's been selected from a range of sources and presented in digestible 'chunks' to mildly entertain or pass the time for the reader. The audience is broad: adult, intrigued by fascinating facts, sharing a Western culture. The article can appear only in a very general publication available to such an audience, in this case *Cara*, the complimentary Aer Lingus in-flight magazine.

Pulling apart this text makes clear how it was written. You can picture the writer at his computer, he is stimulated by the caffeine to write about coffee, he finds a quotation using jargon from a book for connoisseurs, he finds the origin of the word in his dictionary, and he chooses some historical facts from an encyclopaedia or an internet web site. The whole text is made cohesive by his individual voice. This is not to say that such writing is easy. Writing for a wide audience is often more difficult than writing for a very specific one. In this case it's a most professional piece of writing that is perfectly acceptable to its target audience.

ACTIVITY 67

1 On your own, find two further examples of magazines that are aimed at as wide an audience as possible. Examine one article from each and list the assumptions that the writer has made about the shared background, values and culture of the audience.

2 In small groups you should compare your findings and note any recurring similarities.
3 In larger groups or as a class, discuss whether any minority groups within society would be excluded from finding the texts acceptable. Why?

COMMENTARY

On Text 47

Some of the points you should have noted under your headings:

1 *Uncertainty*
   - Words and phrases from a semantic field of possibility and vagueness are frequent: 'likely', 'chance', 'a little more', 'seems', 'a bit up and down', 'opportunity'.
   - Use of conditional clauses, ie clauses suggesting certain options that affect future events: 'If you need to ...', 'if you grasp ...', 'If you have to ...'.
   - Generalised comments and descriptions that could mean anything: 'A time of change', 'figures of authority'.
   - Many verbs have their basic meaning altered or 'modified' by the insertion of words like 'may', 'should', and 'could'. The effect is to introduce elements of doubt, probability or possibility into simple statements of fact: 'you may feel', 'You should have', 'there could be'.

2 *Certainty*
   - Sentences are either declaratives or imperatives, giving the impression of either stating facts or directing your positive actions: 'A time of change is approaching', or 'Give yourself a break'.
   - Words and phrases from a semantic field of certainty: 'make sure', 'double-check'.
   - The jargon of astrology implies the specialist knowledge of the writer: 'Mercury in retrograde', 'When Venus and Mars move into Aquarius'.
   - Mode includes several aspects of speech: elision ('you're', 'Don't'); colloquialisms ('get', 'fall into place', 'ironed out'); frequent imperatives 'make the most of', 'make sure'); personal reference ('yourself'). The writer appears to speak to you like a trusted friend, sharing your concern about things that matter to you – relationships, money and work.
   - Graphologically, the regular 'personal challenge' section, foregrounded by bold font, reinforces the personal address to the reader.
   - The writer's technique – their 'stylistic fingerprints' – has already become clear from this analysis. By a careful choice of linguistic features, the writer has woven a text that superficially provides positive guidance and encouragement, even though it has no real substance.

COMMENTARY

On Text 55

These observations aren't intended as a complete analysis or answer to all of the activity questions. They simply highlight some important aspects that will help you in future analysis.

   - Structure is a basic and repeated question/answer format.
   - You apparently read (or 'hear') only the words spoken. No additional comments are made by the interviewer.
   - As you read, you may well assume that you are reading everything that was said, in the order that it was said. There is nothing to show whether the sequence has been altered or omissions made.
   - Gillespie's answers must have been edited to remove the more

distracting aspects of spontaneous speech (false starts, fillers, pauses, etc). In contrast, some aspects of speech, such as elision, have been retained for their more natural sound. The whole interview has obviously been 'tidied up' to make it coherent and readable.

■ At this point you may be wondering how much, if any, of the original interview has been reproduced, and how much rewritten in a style that the magazine knows will be acceptable to its target audience. In fact, the whole text *could* have been created by the magazine, and then shown to Gillespie for his approval of the content.

COMMENTARY
On Text 54

■ Structure is far more complicated. It is not a simple question/answer format.

■ Within the first few lines it becomes clear that the sequence of the material has been altered (the opening quotation occurred some way into the interview), and that cuts have been made (eg much of the opening 40 minutes).

■ Distracting elements of speech have been edited out, but a greater naturalness is achieved through graphology (italics for stress, and exclamation mark), as well as by elision and taboo language.

■ The interviewer's presence and his interpretation of events are very apparent. This needs detailed analysis:

a The writer describes from his own point of view how Cantrell speaks: 'bristles', 'sighs', 'swiftly adds', etc.

b He adds, in parenthesis, extra information needed for the reader's full understanding: '(Staley, A/C singer)' and '(drug)'.

c He makes critical comments both on what Cantrell says: 'On the contrary . . .' and doesn't say: 'Cantrell isn't about to . . .'.

d The reader appears to 'see' the writer through Cantrell's eyes: 'Until now, the *Kerrang!* journalist . . . heroin addiction'.

e The writer appears to collaborate with the reader in the interview by confiding his interview strategy: 'So we'll stick . . . *Alice In Chains*'. Consequently, the reader is intrigued to discover whether this ploy works.

These separate observations can now be summarised. Conventionally, you imagine an interview as a repeated question and answer sequence. Even though interviews are frequently more complex and varied, you nevertheless expect to hear that sequence or see that structure on the page. In its basic form, then, such an interview structure looks accurate and complete, as you appear to hear only the actual words spoken. But in this form the interview can be dissatisfying for the reader. You hear the words, but you lack any detailed knowledge of the context. It is hard to visualise the full situation; depth and colour are missing.

The *Kerrang!* journalist has woven a far more sophisticated pattern of words. He has added variety and colour to the selected interview quotations, not only by involving himself, but also by constantly altering the point from which the reader sees what's going on. Sometimes you seem to be in the mind of the interviewee, sometimes in the mind of the interviewer, and sometimes (as in 'Had Cantrell always fancied doing a solo album?') you feel somehow you are in both.

In this last example the journalist's actual question would have been *'Have you* always fancied doing a solo album?' He would report it simply as 'I *asked if Cantrell had* always fancied doing a solo album'. The version in the text is a strange mixture of the two. It omits the reporting introduction, changes the word order to that of a question ('Cantrell had' becomes 'Had Cantrell',) and adds a question mark as if it was a real question. Deliberate confusion of the grammar causes a similar confusion in the reader's mind. You may not be sure of your point of view, but you have become very involved in the text! This particular device, called **free indirect discourse**, is more frequently found in fiction, but you should not be surprised to meet it in any text that includes elements of story structure (eg biography, travelogue, interview).

In their own ways both interviews use language to manipulate the target audience into accepting a particular version of events. It isn't possible to calculate just how accurate, truthful or complete each text is. Of course, it may not be too important in these examples, but accounts of interviews with politicians and others in positions of power or authority are another matter.

ACTIVITY 68

1 Find an interview in any magazine you read regularly. Examine the way it is recounted: to what extent does it appear to be an objective record or a subjective evaluation? What techniques of language does the writer use to convey any personal opinion?

2 Write up your analysis and assess the effectiveness of the writer's style.

3 Rewrite Text 55 by using some of the techniques used by the *Kerrang!* journalist. (You will, of course, need to be inventive!) How has this rewriting changed the purposes of the text?

By analysing magazine texts you have learnt how:

- modal verbs and modality affect the meaning of a passage in which they occur by suggesting meanings that can include possibility, probability and permission etc
- euphemism works to make what might be offensive acceptable
- dysphemism is used to offend or embarrass an audience.

Further reading:

Seeing Through Language by Ronald Carter & Walter Nash. Blackwell (1990). An accessible and clear guide to the ways in which language is used in magazines, newspapers and advertising.

7 The Nuisance of Newspapers

In this chapter you will examine a variety of newspaper extracts to discover their purposes and their variations in writing style. Like a magazine each contains numerous smaller texts, many of which share superficial similarities of house style in layout conventions, fonts, and so on. But there are often crucial differences not only between newspapers but also between texts within the pages of one paper. You will discover the features of language that make newspaper writing peculiarly unique, and you will develop your grammatical understanding of the sentence.

Newspapers have always aroused strong feelings, whether intentionally or not. Over two hundred years ago in his satirical comedy *The Critic*, Sheridan has one of his characters say, 'The newspapers! Sir, they are the most villainous – licentious – abominable – infernal – Not that I ever read them – no – I make it a rule never to look into a newspaper.' You may feel nothing much has changed, but however you react to them, they remain an important and influential form of communication, even in this age of instant electronic interaction. Looking into them should therefore be enlightening.

Texts in newspapers

Very broadly, newspapers contain three main types of text: reports of news events; opinion about those events; and advertising. Reports of news may include background information; opinion may be in the form of an editorial (the paper's own view), a column by a regular contributor, or letters to the editor; advertising may be in the normal full display form or in abbreviated small print 'classifieds'.

The following extract reports a complete news event (the omitted final section listed some of the injured). It's tempting to see the first text in a chapter as an example of either good or bad practice, so to avoid this it has been chosen deliberately as an example of a journalistic style no longer used. This will allow you to get to grips with the purpose and style, rather than take it as the norm by which to judge others. It will also reveal something about the structure of news events. The report comes from *The Times* of 15 July 1852.

TEXT 56

DREADFUL RAILWAY ACCIDENT.
BURNLEY, JULY 13.

Yesterday morning several monster excursion trains left Burnley, conveying upwards of 5,000 of the teachers, children, and friends of the various Sunday schools of the town to York, Goole, Liverpool, and other places. The Goole train, engaged by the Wesleyan Methodists, consisted of about 35 carriages, containing some 1,200 persons, and reached Burnley, on its return, about 11.30 p.m., every one delighted with the day's trip to the sea, and quite unprepared for the most fearful railway accident which has ever occurred in this neighbourhood. The train had arrived within a few hundred yards of the station, when it was brought to a stand for the purpose of detaching the engines (according to the usual practice), and running the train on to the main line, which is not employed at this station for the ordinary passenger traffic; but before the engines could be disposed of the train, from its weight, was again in motion, and, before the pointsman could attend to his duty, had passed on, down the incline, to the usual passenger platform, which is adapted only for a short train, and terminates in a strong stone wall. The train entered the station with considerable impetus, and dashed against the buffers protecting the wall, two of the carriages being raised completely on end, and almost shivered to pieces by the concussion. The scene which ensued was most lamentable, and almost baffles description, the screams of mothers for their children being mingled with the cries and groans of the wounded. The news of the calamity soon spread through the town, and the confusion was increased by the hundreds of people who crowded into the station. Mr. Superintendent Carswell, with a party of the county constabulary, was soon on the spot, and resorted to active measures for the extrication of the injured, four of whom were found to be quite dead, and some 20 or 30 seriously injured.

A special engine was despatched to Manchester immediately after the accident for Mr. Hall, the passenger superintendent, who arrived at 3 o'clock this morning. After a careful investigation of the circumstances, Mr. Hall is of opinion, that had the points been properly attended to the accident would not have occurred. The pointsman (John Parker) is in custody, and an inquest will be held on the bodies tomorrow.

ACTIVITY 69

1 In small groups, identify the features of language that make up the individual register of the text. You should pay particular attention to the structure of the whole text and of the separate sentences (note for example the subject of each sentence), the content and the lexis. Nominate one person to record your analysis of the tenor and purpose, and include examples to support your view.

2 In large groups or as a class, compare your analyses. Choose one feature that you think more than any other accounts for the difference in reporting style between then and now.

When you have completed the activity, you should read the observations at the end of this chapter. These in turn introduce the next section on grammar.

Sentence first – verdict afterwards

The crucial unit or 'chunk' of meaning in written language is the sentence. Words may supply much of the colour to a text, but it's the sentence that organises these words and their colours to create a particular pattern. Writers display their individual stylistic fingerprints most clearly by the type and variety of sentence structure that they choose. Whole books have been written on the sentence (after all, grammar is largely about the sentence); this book can only outline some basic structures and recommend you develop your knowledge by further reading and practice in analysis. You will then be better informed to make judgements about a writer's style.

In its basic form the sentence uses one verb to say something that is complete and self-contained between capital letter and full stop. So:

a 'Boris drank the vodka.'

> This is a **simple sentence**: It contains a subject ('Boris') and it says something about him. It is perfectly understandable and makes complete sense. The fact that you don't know the identity of Boris is irrelevant. 'He drank it' is a complete sentence, even though you don't know who or what is referred to. You could lengthen (**a**) by describing Boris, the vodka, how he drank it and so on, but it remains a simple sentence for as long as it contains only one main verb:

b 'Boris the old gardener quickly drank the fiery home-made vodka.'

> Simple sentences tend to be fairly short. One way of lengthening a sentence is to join two previously separate sentences together. So, if you add:

c 'Ivan devoured the caviar.' to **a**:
d 'Boris drank the vodka and Ivan devoured the caviar.',

> you have one sentence but two main verbs that each indicate who did something. The Simple Sentence has become a **multiple sentence**, and so that you can discuss the two parts, each previously separate unit or sentence is now referred to as a **clause**. (In fact, you can say that a simple sentence is also one clause).
>
> Sentence (**d**) is a particular kind of multiple sentence called a **compound sentence**, and theoretically you could add further units or chunks that say something about a whole collection of people. The point about a compound sentence is that each of the separate clauses within it is independent of the others. Each makes complete sense by itself whether or not it is joined to another clause, and each is of (roughly) equal importance. The link between each clause is usually a **coordinating conjunction** or **coordinator**: a word like 'and', 'or' and 'but' that puts the clauses together in order.
>
> However, it is possible to lengthen (**a**) in another way, by adding a clause that doesn't make complete sense by itself:

e <u>'When he returned home</u> Boris drank the vodka.'

> Here 'When he returned home', though it contains a verb saying when and who did something, nevertheless cannot stand alone. It depends on the **independent** (or **main**) **clause** to explain what action followed the return, and not surprisingly is therefore called a **dependent clause**. This more complicated sentence is called a **complex** sentence. Again, it would be possible to expand it by adding further dependent clauses, none of which is complete by itself:

f <u>'When he returned home</u> Boris drank the vodka, <u>so that he might forget the terrible deed.</u>'

> Here, certain additional information describing the time and Boris' reason for drinking is conveyed by two dependent clauses. They are also frequently referred to as **subordinate clauses** because they contain chunks of information that are considered somewhat less important than the main clause. Words or phrases that introduce such clauses are called **subordinating conjunctions** or **subordinators**. They introduce information about such matters as time ('after', 'while', 'before'), place

('where'), reason ('because'), purpose ('so as to'), result ('so that'), and conditions ('if', 'unless').

One most common and useful type of dependent clause is the **relative clause**, a clause that adds further description about a person or thing just mentioned. They are introduced by **relative pronouns** (eg 'who', 'which', 'that'): words that relate back to the person or thing about to be described. So, for instance:

g 'Boris, <u>who had a severe hangover,</u> drank the vodka <u>that he had hidden in the potting shed'</u>.

Finally, it is common to lengthen sentences by combining a compound sentence with one or more dependent clauses, creating a **compound-complex sentence**:

h 'When he returned home Boris drank the vodka and Ivan devoured the caviar.'

You can of course add further dependent clauses to describe the place, reason, result, etc.

So:　　　one independent clause = simple sentence
　　　　　two or more clauses = multiple sentence, of which three types exist:
　　　　　a two or more independent clauses = compound sentence
　　　　　b one independent (main) + 1 or more dependent (subordinate) clauses = complex sentence
　　　　　c two or more independent (main) + 1 or more dependent (subordinate) clauses = compound-complex sentence

This is a basic outline for possible variations in structure. The clauses themselves can vary in form, function, and sequence; the links between them can be equally diverse. But even this elementary framework allows you to make observations about Text 56 that reveal more than that the sentences are merely 'long and complicated'. Of the ten sentences, none is a simple sentence, number 10 is compound, numbers 1, 8 and 9 complex, and numbers 2–7 compound-complex.

If, for example, you examine some of the links between the clauses in sentence 3 ('when', 'for the purpose of', 'which', 'but before', 'before', 'which'), you find that they provide different sorts of information to expand on the opening main clause: 'The train had arrived within a few hundred yards of the station'.

They give details of time, reasons, causes, and relevant railway procedures. A carefully interlinked description has been composed to explain how and why this accident occurred. The writer's meaning is apparent not simply from his choice of vocabulary but from his choice of structure. Now that you have the basics, any investment you make in further study of grammatical structures will repay you soundly in analytical understanding. Examples of suitable books are listed at the end of this chapter.

You will return to Text 56 shortly. In the meantime, here are the opening paragraphs from two different newspapers reporting the same story. The first extract is from the *Daily Telegraph* (DT), the second from the *Daily Record* (DR). They both appeared on the front page, the headlines being respectively:

'Clinton strikes terrorist bases' (DT) and 'LIAR BILL GOES FOR HIS GUN' (DR).

TEXT 57

Daily Telegraph

THE UNITED States launched military strikes in Afghanistan and Sudan yesterday against centres allegedly linked with the terrorist bombings of two American embassies.

Gen Henry Shelton, chairman of the Joint Chiefs of Staff, said further military operations were being considered. The threat posed by terrorists meant no details would be given in case they endangered the lives of US troops.

Eye witnesses in Sudan said at least two aircraft were involved in a series of bombing runs over the factory near Khartoum although it is likely that cruise missiles were used in Afghanistan. There were no initial indications of the extent of the damage but President Clinton issued a defiant statement saying: 'Today, we have struck back.'

He ordered the American military to carry out attacks against six training bases in Afghanistan and a factory in Sudan believed to be producing components for chemical weapons.

Breaking off his holiday in Martha's Vineyard to fly to Washington, the President said he ordered the offensive after 'compelling information' that further attacks against US targets were being planned. He called a surprise press conference to announce the offensive which he said had been planned and carried out successfully in complete secrecy.

TEXT 58

Daily Record

EMBATTLED Bill Clinton last night used his military muscle to avenge the US Embassy bombings.

The scandal-hit President sent stealth bombers to attack Islamic terror targets in Sudan and Afghanistan.

The strikes came as Monica Lewinsky accused Clinton of lying about their affair, and opponents demanded his impeachment.

Sites used by millionaire Saudi dissident Osama bin Laden were among the targets. Bin Laden is widely believed to have masterminded the attacks on US embassies in Kenya and Tanzania which killed 257 people on August 7.

White House sources said Clinton approved the attacks last Friday, and sat up with his advisers until 3am yesterday discussing when to strike.

The US attacked seven targets in Afghanistan, including a terrorist compound described as among the world's most active.

ACTIVITY 70

1 In small groups, examine the way in which each text reports this news item. Groups should concentrate on *either* similarities *or* differences in the ways that language is used. Nominate one person from each group to record the similarities or differences with textual examples. Particular features you should analyse are lexis, sentence and paragraph structure, and narrative structure.

2 In larger groups or as a class, compare and discuss your lists. Do some features occur as both similarities *and* differences? Can you explain these satisfactorily? Why do the differences that you have detected exist? How different are the purposes intended by each writer?

Before continuing with these activities, you should now read the observations on the two texts at the end of this chapter.

3 In small groups, re-examine the events recounted in each version, and place them in chronological order. (You may need to split some sentences into separate clauses to do this accurately.)

4 Re-write the story from either the *Daily Telegraph* or the *Daily Record*, keeping to the chronological order of events and retaining as much of the original wording as you can. How effective is your version? What problems did you have producing it?

Looking from the gutter

Of course, some tabloid papers deserve their reputation for sensationalism and trivialisation. Here is part of a news item from the *Sun* that typifies the extremes possible in journalese. The full story comprised 15 paragraphs, while the rest of the page was almost entirely taken up with photographs of Perry Southall and Clarence Morris, and related items on Morris' background and the current law.

TEXT 59

Scandal of stalker 'too crazy' to lock up
PSYCHO'S GOING TO KILL ME
Terror of stunning Pammi lookalike

By BRIAN FLYNN and ANDREA BUSFIELD

SOBBING Pamela Anderson lookalike Perry Southall told of her terror last night after the psycho who has made her life hell was deemed TOO MAD to lock up.

The stunning blonde, 22, gasped in court as crazed stalker Clarence Morris was told he could walk free. Later she wept: 'I'm afraid he's out to kill me.'

The amazing ruling came after a psychiatrist pronounced the convicted child-rapist 'untreatable.'

Exasperated judge Peter Fingret said that meant he was powerless to send Morris to an asylum. As MPs and victims' groups last night blasted the astonishing loophole that let the fiend back on the streets, Perry said: 'Do I have to be murdered before the lesson is learned? *He is a walking timebomb. I feel absolutely numb and utterly let down by the law.*'

Infatuated Morris, who menaced Perry with a claw-hammer as he stalked her for eight months, will live just **TWO MILES** from her new home in Wanstead, East London. Cops have given her a panic button to carry. She said:

'I'm too scared to go out of my front door knowing he is free.

I hope the psychiatrist will be able to live with himself if I am attacked or he stabs another victim.

Defiance

'Now I have become the prisoner and he is free to do what he wants. If he does not get me, I'm sure he will get someone else.'

Morris had been in custody since September 1996 when he was convicted of assaulting the frightened dental nurse.

ACTIVITY 71

1 In small groups, list with examples the main features of this type of journalese. You should pay particular attention to graphology, lexis (including clichés), selection of facts and narrative structure. What is the effect of these features in combination? What purpose do the quotations serve? Do you think any are genuine?

2 In small groups, rewrite the text as you think it would appear in the *Daily Telegraph* or another broadsheet you are familiar with. What changes have you had to make in the way you have used language?

3 Exchange your final version with that of another group and assess how successful is their rewrite.

ACTIVITY 72

Rewrite Text 56 as it might appear today in *either* a broadsheet *or* a tabloid. You should remember that the original 1852 report already represents the result of a selection process – you don't have access to the 'whole' event. You may therefore need to be suitably inventive!

ACTIVITY 73

Bring into class as many newspapers as you can from one single day. In groups, choose one story that appears in two or three papers (depending on the time available) and compare the ways in which it is treated. What is the main purpose of the story in each paper? Draw up a detailed audience profile for each paper based on your analyses.

Pressed into service

Two closely-related aspects of journalese that explain a great deal about the daily process of journalism are the opening paragraph and the headline. The writer Rudyard Kipling, who began his career as a reporter, captured the essence of the news story in his rhyme:

> I keep six honest serving-men
> (They taught me all I knew);
> Their names are What and Why and When
> And How and Where and Who.

Without the answers to these, you have no news. Not only that, they should all appear in the first paragraph of the story, compressed into as few words as possible. The journalist aims for this ideal account each time he writes a news item. Look again at the opening paragraph of Text 59. It tells you who ('Pamela Anderson lookalike Perry Southall'), what ('told of her terror'), when ('last night'), how ('Sobbing'), and why ('after the psycho' etc). In this case the 'where' is not immediately so important. Or Text 57: who ('The United States'), what ('launched military strikes ... against centres') – note that 'strikes' implies 'how', where ('in Afghanistan and Sudan'), when ('yesterday'), and why ('allegedly linked with ...' etc).

Why this compression of the story into the first paragraph? The simple answer is that at the time of writing a story the reporter can't know how much room will be available in the paper. The editor will make that decision based on what else he wants to include. As there will be no time to rewrite stories, it is simplest if the editor shortens a story 'from the bottom up'. This means that the most ruthless editor who leaves only the opening paragraph still manages to publish the whole story, even if it is in an extremely summarised form. This process explains the strange 'instalment method' structure of the whole story. Increasingly greater details are placed later in the story so that their possible loss won't affect the basic report. It doesn't take long to realise that this whole process has one further effect. A journalist will ensure that his opening presents the story in terms of what he sees as most relevant and important.

The constant aim of such concentration in meaning has also affected the structure of newspaper sentences. The grammatical subjects are often phrased so that a great deal of description is placed before the person or object in question. Returning to Text 59, the subject Perry Southall is described as 'Sobbing Pamela Anderson lookalike' *before* her name is mentioned. Grammatically, a more conventional way would be to write something like, 'Perry Southall, who was sobbing and looks very like Pamela Anderson...', but this shows just how peculiar it is to link such diverse facts. Here the writer has selected two aspects he believes are important, and he foregrounds them accordingly. As you read the story, you meet further examples of this 'cramming' of facts and description before or immediately following the noun: 'The stunning blonde, 22', 'crazed stalker Clarence Morris', 'Exasperated judge, Peter Fingret', and so on. This process of clustering so much information around a noun can be described in several ways, but one will be enough here. Any description that precedes a noun can be called **premodification**; in other words, the noun is developed or 'modified' by further details placed in front of it. Likewise any description appearing after the noun is **postmodification**. 'The stunning (*premodification*) blonde, 22 (*postmodification*)' includes examples of both kinds of modification. Journalists frequently use a particularly concentrated variety of modification in order to state in the opening of their sentences the aspects they believe are significant.

If the first paragraph is a compressed summary of the story, then the headline is a compressed summary of the first paragraph. This need to express in a headline so much meaning in so few words explains its unnatural and contorted structure, particularly on the front page where grabbing attention is crucial. Large font size is helpful here, which of course is why tabloids use simple words: the shorter they are, the bigger they can be printed.

ACTIVITY 74

1 In pairs, re-examine Texts 57 and 58 for examples of concentrated modification. Which kind of modification is used predominantly? What difference do you detect between the two texts?

2 In groups of two or three, examine two stories from at least two current newspapers.

How does the first paragraph answer the six basic questions? To what extent has modification of nouns been necessary to cram the answers into the first sentence or two? How does the headline summarise the first paragraph?

ACTIVITY 75

Write a story based on a recent incident, in the journalese of a named newspaper – broadsheet or tabloid. Incorporate as many features of the appropriate style as possible, and use no more than 250 words.

Features

Features are articles written by journalists, often freelance, about matters of general interest. The following feature appeared in the science news page of the *Independent* on 12 November 1997. It represents an update on research that the editor believes will interest a significant number of readers.

TEXT 60
Revealed: the sweet smell of girls' success at exams

Success in exams may be something to be sniffed at after all. Psychologists have discovered that smell-association is a powerful aid to memory for students, particularly among those who are anxious or apprehensive. The researchers found that students exposed to various unusual background smells while trying to absorb large chunks of text or data, were able to remember much more when exposed to the same smell at the time of recall. When compared to the performance of students who had not been exposed to such smells, the volunteers were able to recall almost 20 per cent more of the text they had tried to remember.

The research of Dr Rachel Herz, reported in *The Psychologist* this week, opens up a whole new area of opportunity for students. The aromas of peppermint, violet leaf and pine were used in the experiment, but Dr Herz of the Monell Chemical Senses Center in Philadelphia says that smell-association will only work as a memory aid if the odour is either unusual, like a new perfume, or out of context, like chocolate in a laboratory.

'Sure it will work, but only if it is new and unusual. Go to a perfume department, pick out something you have never smelt before, put it on the desk while you are studying for your test, and then bring it in with you a few days later when you are doing the test and it will work,' she said.

In a series of studies, Dr Herz set up experiments in the presence or absence of a smell. 'The subjects were taken to a room with an ambient odour and they learnt a series of words. They were then brought back to another room a few days or a week later and some were exposed to the same odour and some not. What we found was that memory is significantly affected by the specific odour,' she said.

ACTIVITY 76

1 Rewrite the article (including a headline) as it might appear in the *Sun*, in no more than 150 words.
2 Discuss the reasons for your selection of facts and adopted style of writing.
3 How does the original article differ in structure and use of language from a news story?

Review

In this chapter you have examined not only the peculiarities of some newspaper writing but also the reasons, historical and ideological, that account for them. The reporting of current news events varies in style depending on the particular paper, but the reports also share much in common. Whatever style is adopted, it usually remains absolutely impersonal; you are never aware of an individual voice speaking to you. This is not true of editorials, regular columns or features, such as Texts 61 and 62. As with many magazines, newspapers contain a variety of writing that appeals to the wider interests of the readers. Again they are collections of texts, bound together by a set of general assumptions about shared beliefs and values. For further practice in analysis here are two contrasting texts. Sample examination scripts discussing them are reviewed in Chapter 9.

The following text is a complete feature article that appeared in the *Daily Mirror* on 13 July 1955, the day on which Ruth Ellis, the last woman to be executed in Great Britain for murder, was hanged.

TEXT 61

The woman who hangs today

It's a fine day for haymaking. A fine day for fishing. A fine day for lolling in the sunshine. And if you feel that way – and I mourn to say that millions of you do – it's a fine day for a hanging.

IF YOU READ THIS BEFORE NINE O'CLOCK THIS MORNING, the last dreadful and obscene preparations for hanging Ruth Ellis will be moving up to their fierce and sickening climax. The public hangman and his assistant will have been slipped into the prison at about four o'clock yesterday afternoon.

There, from what is grotesquely called 'some vantage point' and unobserved by Ruth Ellis, they will have spied upon her when she was at exercise 'to form an impression of the physique of the prisoner'.

A bag of sand will have been filled to the same weight as the condemned woman and it will have been left hanging overnight to stretch the rope.

IF YOU READ THIS AT NINE O'CLOCK, then – short of a miracle – you and I and every man and woman in the land with head to think and heart to feel will, in full responsibility, blot this woman out.

The hands that place the white hood over her head will not be our hands. But the guilt – and guilt there is in all this abominable business – will belong to us as much as to the wretched executioner paid and trained to do the job in accordance with the savage public will.

* * *

IF YOU READ THIS AFTER NINE O'CLOCK, the murderess, Ruth Ellis, will have gone.

The one thing that brings stature and dignity to mankind and raises us above the beasts of the field will have been denied her – pity and the hope of ultimate redemption. The medical officer will go to the pit under the trap door to see that life is extinct. Then in the barbarous wickedness of this ceremony, rejected by nearly all civilised peoples, the body will be left to hang for one hour.

IF YOU READ THESE WORDS OF MINE AT MIDDAY the grave will have been dug while there are no prisoners around and the Chaplain will have read the burial service after he and all of us have come so freshly from disobeying the Sixth Commandment which says 'Thou shalt not kill.'

The secrecy of it all shows that if compassion is not in us, then at least we still retain the dregs of shame. The medieval notice of execution will have been posted on the prison gates and the usual squalid handful of louts and rubbernecks who attend these legalised killings will have had their own private obscene delights.

* * *

Two Royal Commissions have protested against these horrible events. Every Home Secretary in recent years has testified to the agonies of his task, and the revulsion he has felt towards his duty. None has ever claimed that executions prevent murder.

Yet they go on and still Parliament has neither the resolve nor the conviction, nor the wit, nor the decency to put an end to these atrocious affairs.

When I write about capital punishment, as I have often done, I get some praise and usually more abuse. In this case I have been reviled as being a 'sucker for a pretty face.'

Well, I am a sucker for a pretty face. And I am a sucker for all human faces because I hope I am a sucker for all humanity, good or bad. But I prefer the face not to be lolling because of a judicially broken neck.

Yes, it is a fine day.

Oscar Wilde, when he was in Reading Gaol, spoke with melancholy of 'that little tent of blue which prisoners call the sky'.

The tent of blue should be dark and sad at the things we have done this day.

ACTIVITY 77

In small groups, identify the ways in which language is used effectively in this text. Use the framework for analysis questions to establish the register. You should pay particular attention to the use of lexis (including semantic fields, denotation and connotation), graphology, organisation of ideas and overall structure, and grammar (including use of passive voice and pronouns). What purposes does the writer intend this article to serve?

This text is discussed further in Chapter 9.

By contrast, here is a tabloid news feature discussing the confrontation of party leaders in June 1997. This was the first time that the leader of the Labour Government, Tony Blair, and the recently-elected Conservative Opposition Leader, William Hague, had faced each other in debate on the floor of the House of Commons.

TEXT 62

BLAIR VERSUS HAGUE: ROUND ONE
The boy William did well

By MATTHEW PARRIS
Ex-Tory MP and Political Columnist

To call young William Hague stressed, at 2.59 in the Commons yesterday afternoon, would be to understate. He was wetting his knickers.

It was young William's first day as leader of his gang. Unfortunately, Master Hague's mum could not come with him into the Commons playground.

He was left alone, just before three o'clock, to face the leader of the rival gang: the youth they call 'Tony'.

How would he do? All his gang turned up to support him, and Tony's gang, which is more than twice as big, crowded in, blocked the doors and stood in the aisles.

William was scared. From our seats in the press gallery above we could see him twitching and fidgeting with his notes. He knew he had to square up to Tony and all eyes would be on him when he did. Playtime lasts half an hour. William could pick his moment. If he had been cooler he would have waited. But he had to get this over with, and the sooner the better.

Froth

Sitting on the edge of his seat, he was so wound up he almost rose to his feet before Premier Blair even had time to answer the first question.

Which was from a Wolverhampton Labour MP, Dennis Turner.

Turner did not wish to ask about the G8 Summit in Denver, the Earth Summit in New York, the Chancellor's plans for City Regulation, or the future of old age pensions. He wanted to ask about beer.

Specifically, did the Prime Minister agree that beer should come in 'a full pint with the froth on top?'

Thank you, Wolverhampton.

Tony hardly had time to agree before young William rocketed up and, clutching the dispatch box, launched into a volley of questions about whether or not the Labour Party in Wales was persecuting Labour MPs who disagree with the Government's plans for a Welsh Assembly.

William said one MP had been threatened with the sack. Tony said he hadn't. *William said he had.* Tony said he hadn't. *William said he had.* Tony said he hadn't. *William said he had.* Tony said he hadn't.

Five times the lads traded accusations. The Tory gang cheered William and the Labour gang cheered Tony. And nobody was any the wiser.

All we can say is that William sounded terrified, but stuck to his guns; and Tony sounded confident, but looked mightily irked.

Better

I was once an MP, and I watched Margaret Thatcher, then John Major, and now Tony Blair take Questions for the first time as Prime Minister. And I watched Jim Callaghan, then Michael Foot, then Neil Kinnock, then John Smith, and then Tony Blair try their hand, as Opposition Leaders, asking them.

And I think both William and Tony got off to a better start than most. Maybe Commons playtime isn't going to be as boring as we feared.

ACTIVITY 78

'How does the writer use language to influence the reader's view of the two political leaders?' Write an answer to this question. Include some analysis of semantic fields, graphology and tenor.

This text is discussed further in Chapter 9.

COMMENTARY

On Text 56

Some of the features you should have noticed:

- Graphology: very little font variation (upper case italics for headline); only two paragraphs; much punctuation.
- The headline itself is not strongly emotive.
- Most sentences seem long and complicated – ten in all ranging from 17 to 103 words (six between 23 and 33 words).
- All declarative sentences.
- Passive voice is often used, eg: 'confusion <u>was increased</u>', 'A special engine <u>was despatched</u>', 'four of whom <u>were found</u> to be quite dead', '<u>had</u> the points <u>been</u> properly <u>attended</u> to'. This construction functions either to maintain focus on the main event or to avoid pinning responsibility on any one person. So, in the above examples: 'confusion' reinforces the earlier 'calamity'; it would give too much prominence to

the onlookers if the active were used, eg: 'and hundreds of people crowded into the station, increasing the confusion'. To name the persons responsible for despatching the engine or pronouncing victims dead would also be distracting and unnecessary; to identify a person responsible for not attending to the points (possibly John Parker) would prejudice any future investigation and could be libellous.

- The grammatical subjects of the sentences maintain a focus on the train, the disaster in general, and persons of responsibility: 'excursion trains', 'The Goole train', 'The train', 'The train', 'The scene', 'The news of the calamity', 'Mr. Superintendent Carswell', 'A special engine', 'Mr. Hall', and 'The pointsman'.
- The text appears highly factual at the expense of subjective opinion or expression of emotion. The few exceptions are generalised and stereotypical, eg: 'delighted with the day's trip', 'most lamentable', 'screams of mothers for their children being mingled with the cries and groans of the wounded'.
- The lexis doesn't appear colloquial. It is generally literate and educated, the more unusual words in this context (eg: 'concussion', 'extrication') explainable by the changes in language use over the last 150 years.
- The readers are not directly addressed or referred to.

Overall, the tone is serious and impersonal; the extremely factual method of recounting makes it sound authoritative and believable. For its target audience the level of formality would have been deliberative (but of course any piece written in this style today would be frozen). As to its main purpose, it certainly isn't to express the individual suffering of the victims. The focus is very much on the events leading up to the accident and its possible cause. It's enough for the moment to appreciate this difference in focus between an earlier time and now. However, it's worth adding that you would be rash to see the text as concerned merely with facts for their own sake and not people. Railways were still expanding rapidly in the 1850s; they were a source of employment, wealth, pride and corruption. Railways were news, reflecting social and political concerns, and this particular account has selected certain facts to highlight some of those concerns.

The key feature that makes the text so different from a modern account is the narrative structure. The event is told in a purely chronological order, as it happened, from the time the train left Burnley to the placing of the pointsman in custody. The consecutive subjects of the ten sentences, previously identified, clearly display this sequence. Even today we speak of the 'news story' – originally told as you would tell a story in its simplest form: from beginning to end. What seems natural in everyday story telling now seems unnatural in newspaper format.

COMMENTARY

On Texts 57 and 58

The following observations are deliberately selective in order to stimulate discussion; you may well have noticed other features.

Lexis
Similarities:

- Both share vocabulary from the semantic field of war: 'military', 'strikes', 'bombings', 'attacks', 'terrorist'.
- Both use emotive language to describe actions: 'defiant' (DT); 'terror targets', 'scandal-hit' (DR).

Differences:

- DT uses greater variety of synonyms: 'strikes', 'operations', 'bombing runs', 'attacks', 'offensive'.
- DT uses proportionally more educated, literate and polysyllabic lexis: 'military operations', 'initial indications', 'compelling information'.
- DR uses emotive lexis more often, especially at the beginning, some of it blatantly contrived to arouse feeling: 'military muscle', 'avenge', 'scandal-hit', 'stealth bombers', 'terror targets', 'terrorist compound'.
- DR uses alliteration to dramatise aspects: 'military muscle', 'terror targets'.
- DR uses **clichés**: 'military muscle', 'masterminded'.
- Relative formality of address differs: 'The United States' and 'American' (DT) v. 'US' (DR); 'President Clinton' (DT) v. 'Bill Clinton' (DR). DT reinforces the authority of the existing government.
- In first paragraph DT attributes the action to the state; DR attributes it to a familiarised personality. But note the two headlines.

Sentence and paragraph structure
Similarities:

- Declarative sentences, mostly containing two to four clauses.
- Short paragraphs consisting of one or two sentences each.
- Passive voice used occasionally, sometimes to avoid identifying the agents: 'further military operations were being considered' (DT), 'Bin Laden is widely believed' (DR).
- No use of modal verbs to indicate vagueness or uncertainty, though passive voice often achieves this.

Differences:

- DT has longer sentences (17–33 words, average 25), DR shorter (13–23 words, average 18). Clause length also differs relatively.
- DT demonstrates more sophisticated use of tenses to refer to the time of events: 'were being considered', 'would be given', 'had been planned'.
- DT occasionally acknowledges some uncertainty through hedges, 'allegedly', 'it is likely that'. DR in contrast avoids uncertainty by omitting direct comment and suggesting connections: compare the DT's 'centres allegedly linked with' to the DR's 'Sites used by' that avoids specifying the use.

Narrative structure
Similarities:

- Both violate the 'natural' chronological order of telling events.
- Information about events is deliberately broken up and delivered at intervals in isolated chunks. Compare paragraphs one and four in DT, paragraphs one and six in DR. Consequently, the narration is disjointed and lacks grammatical cohesion. Most sentences contain a different

grammatical subject and make no consistent attempt to organise the information in a rational way. Links are made, but in an apparently random manner.

■ Both texts acknowledge reliance on spoken sources, 'Gen Henry. . . said' (DT), 'White House sources said' (DR).

Differences:

■ DT occasionally quotes direct speech, suggesting authenticity.
■ DR's content is more diverse, incorporating sex scandal material. It also repeats recent facts about embassy deaths to arouse negative feelings.

You probably noticed other features, but two such short extracts can't demonstrate anything like the full range of stylistic possibilities. Nevertheless, they are useful as pointers to discussion and further analysis. National newspapers are traditionally divided into the broadsheet and the tabloid, terms which once referred only to their relative sizes. More recently, however, these terms have attracted connotations that separate them in the minds of many. The broadsheet (or quality) paper supposedly informs: it is associated with an audience that is educated, open-minded, and belonging to the higher classes of society. In contrast the tabloid supposedly entertains: it connotes an audience that is poorly educated, prejudiced, and lower class. Such opposed stereotypical labels can only interfere with any serious analysis and understanding, and you should dismiss them immediately.

What do your observations about the two texts tell you? If the stereotypical view is correct you would surely expect fewer similarities and greater differences between the broadsheet *Daily Telegraph* and the tabloid *Daily Record*. The register of news reporting in papers is called **journalese**, and like other registers it can appear in a number of slightly different stylistic varieties to suit its audience and purpose. Journalese in *The Times* will be very different from that found in the *Sun*, but you will also find many points of similarity.

Both the *Daily Telegraph* and the *Daily Record* provide facts in a rapid-fire manner, in short reader-friendly paragraphs whose divisions have no obvious justification. Both report the news story by adding extra facts 'in instalments' to the original brief opening account. In each case the story is dramatised by its compression of facts and its choice of highly charged vocabulary. However, the tabloid does sensationalise its account by its more emotive, exaggerated and suggestive language, which not only expresses a narrower and more simplistic view of events, but also assumes that its readers are of the same opinion. The above observations show that the tabloid certainly makes fewer demands upon its readers. Neither paper, however, reports the news item in a purely objective or impartial way. On the contrary, each uses language to reconstruct events in a way that it believes will be acceptable to its readers, given their assumed beliefs and values. These beliefs and values are in turn reinforced and perpetuated. Language is never neutral.

In this chapter you have learnt about:

- the distinctive features of journalese, the register of news reporting
- the different sentence structures – simple, compound, complex and compound-complex
- pre- and post-modification of nouns.

Further reading:

Rediscover Grammar by David Crystal, Longman (1996). An exceptionally lucid introduction to basic grammar.

Analysing Sentences by Noel Burton-Roberts, Longman (1997). A clear, comprehensive and genuinely entertaining explanation.

Grammar, Structure and Style by Shirley Russell, OUP (1993). Contains a sound chapter on essential grammatical knowledge.

Newspaper Language by Nicholas Bagnall, Focal Press (1993). A basic and enlightening introduction to the way journalists use language.

Language in the News by Roger Fowler, Routledge (1991). A most readable and illuminating account of the ways in which newspaper language manipulates the reader.

8 Eclectic Ads

In this chapter, you will investigate some of the common linguistic techniques used in a variety of advertisements. You will examine the ways in which ads are constructed for particular purposes, and you will reassess the assumptions made about target audiences. You will also take a final look at sentence structure, and conclude with a review of the importance of intertextuality.

Within an affluent society, the advertising industry can exert a powerful influence on both society as a whole and its individual members. An incredible amount of time, money and expertise is invested in this essential component of the commercial world, and it would be extremely naive to believe that the modern consumer (ourselves included) is somehow sophisticated enough to be immune from its effects. Advertising should be taken very seriously.

The language of advertising

To start with, how much can you learn from a close analysis of one car ad?

TEXT 63

A few of my Favorit things

WAKING up in the early hours of a hot, summer's day. NO thought given to shopping or housework. CAUTION thrown to the wind. SWIMMING costumes, towels, buckets, spades and children into the Favorit. FEELING wonderfully relaxed as we speed through its five gears towards the nearest coast. 1.3 litres, and a top speed rather more than the legal limit will get us there in no time. BREAKFAST at a roadside cafe. BACON and eggs sizzling, fresh bread toasting. MUGS of hot piping tea. THE works all round. BACK on the road. THE excitement in the kids' voices as we get closer. BEING the first to see the sea. NOT far now. SAND between the toes. ICE cream dripping down fingers. CRICKET on the beach. PRINCE catching John out. SCONES and jam. THE long, golden sunset. THE slow, reluctant walk arm-in-arm back to the welcoming comfort of our Favorit. PLENTY of room in the back for the kids to snuggle down for the journey home. I still can't quite believe they manage to fit so much in for the price. LISTENING to my favourite album on the stereo. WATCHING the shadows cast by our halogen headlights. TUCKING the children, then ourselves up in bed. WANTING to do it all again tomorrow.

The above wording appeared below a large black and white picture of a young boy and dog silhouetted against the seashore. Below both were a small picture of the car and five lines of 'small print'.

1 In groups of two or three, examine the text carefully. A good place to begin is with the content – divide this into separate sections. Why is the car not the only topic area?
2 Now list the ways in which language is used to influence the reader. Pay special attention to lexis (including semantic fields and connotations), grammar, overall structure and graphology.
3 What characteristics are shared by the target audience? Write up an audience profile. What purposes does this ad fulfil? How do these purposes match the profile you have drawn?
4 In larger groups, compare and discuss your findings. Where would you expect to find this ad?

You should read the observations on this text at the end of this chapter before continuing.

No nonsense!

One of the observations you have just read is that only two sentences in the ad are grammatically complete. What, then, are the others? They are not incomplete in the sense of unfinished, and they obviously all mean something! In Chapter 7 you looked at basic sentence structures, your starting point being the simple sentence: a sentence containing a subject and a verb that together make complete sense. How do other sentences lack sense?

Traditionally, in written English, a number of conditions have to be fulfilled before you can call a string of words a sentence. The subject has to be mentioned (usually as a noun or pronoun) and the verb has to indicate certain things about the action or state being described. Principally, these things are the **tense** (when something happened), the **person** (first, second or third), and the **number** (singular or plural person). Other aspects needn't concern you at this stage; you can learn more about them in the recommended reading at the end of Chapter 7. So, going back to our example sentence:

a 'Boris loves vodka' contains a subject 'Boris' and a verb indicating present tense and, from its final 's', third person singular. (The form 'love' would not match up or 'agree' with a third person singular subject.)
b 'Ivan hated lemonade' similarly contains a subject and a verb indicating past tense, and as there is only one form of the verb ending in 'ed' it will 'agree' with any subject. More complicated verb forms may need agreement elsewhere:
c 'Boris has loved vodka from infancy'.
   Verbs fulfilling these conditions of tense, person and number are called **finite verbs**, and they occur in all simple sentences and in main clauses of more complicated sentences.

However, many dependent or subordinate clauses do not contain finite verbs. Instead they frequently contain a verb in a form that fails to indicate tense, person or number. So:

d 'Walking through the park' does not indicate who is walking or when. It therefore doesn't make complete sense grammatically, and needs a main clause to provide the missing information. So:

e 'Walking through the park, Boris drank a bottle of vodka.'

f 'Walking through the park, I enjoy the fresh air and sunshine.'

g 'Walking through the park, they will see the new duckpond.'

When a verb occurs in a form that is not limited by tense, person and number it is said to be **non-finite**.

If you turn back to Text 63 and examine the verbs in the first few sentences, you find 'Waking up', 'given', 'thrown', 'Feeling', and so on. All are non-finite verbs that fail to specify the 'who' or 'when'. Instead of being explained by a main clause they are enclosed between a capital letter and a full stop. Such sentences are called **minor sentences** because they omit one or both elements crucial to a simple sentence or main clause: a stated subject and a finite verb. The fact that you may be able to work out the 'who' and 'when' from reading the whole text is irrelevant. If those aspects are not explicitly stated then grammatically the sentences are minor. Meaning, thankfully, doesn't depend solely on grammar. You can express what you mean in 'ungrammatical' ways, and in Chapter 3 you saw that many of the rules of written language should not be applied to speech. Minor sentences often occur as elliptical utterances in spoken language, and now increasingly find their way into more informal written texts. Their presence in ads should be no surprise. In Text 63 the effect of so many minor sentences is arguably to produce a feeling of movement and timelessness, untied to particular people.

Reviewing the sentence

Throughout this book you have been accumulating basic information about the sentence. You can now describe its forms (declarative, interrogative, etc), recognise its structure (simple, compound, etc) and distinguish a minor sentence from a grammatically complete one. In so doing you are becoming increasingly aware of the different effects possible, for so much of a writer's style lies in the individual patterning of their sentences.

ACTIVITY 80

1 In pairs, examine Text 63 and find its two complete sentences. What particular function do you think they perform in the text?

a Find as many ads for cars as possible from a variety of magazines.

b In small groups, identify the differences between them which reflect different target audiences. Look closely at the types of lexis, their connotations, and the predominant semantic fields, as well as the ways in which the audience is addressed. To what extent do these differences rely on a stereotypical audience profile?

Exotic holidays

The following two paragraphs are an extract from a holiday brochure introducing Kerala, a state in south-west India.

TEXT 64

There are no high rise buildings, no casinos, no shopping malls, no theatres, but there is so much to offer the traveller with its breathtaking scenery through the backwaters of beautiful lagoon country, its lush mountain regions with spice and tea plantations and the superb sandy beaches backed by thick forests of palm trees. By general Indian standards Kerala is quite an affluent state, with an abundance of natural produce and resources. The people pride themselves on having the highest literacy rate in the country and a high percentage of the population speak fluent English, right down to the most popular idioms!

The food connoisseurs amongst you will be pleased to know that the cuisine in this region is superb, with particularly good vegetarian dishes, not to mention the fresh fish and seafood, but the best news of all, has to be the low cost of living, which means you get more for your pound! Don't expect plush restaurants (although there are a few), but lots of 'shacks' where the food is cooked in the traditional way, is absolutely delicious and served up by the most welcoming of people.

ACTIVITY 81

1 In groups of two or three, analyse the text, paying special attention to the choice of content and lexis, the connotations, and the tenor. What can you deduce about the target audience from this extract? Draw up as detailed a profile as you can.

2 In larger groups compare your profiles. What cultural myth about exotic holidays is reinforced in the ad? Discuss the differences

necessary in rewriting the text for the same audience as an extract for:
a a guide book, and
b a travelogue.

3 On your own, rewrite the text in either of the two genres.

4 In pairs, exchange your versions and assess their relative success.

ACTIVITY 82

1 Collect from brochures and magazines a range of holiday ads that target different audiences (family, 18–30 clubber, retired, camper, etc) and classify them by type.

2 In groups exchange your texts and compare your categories. What features of language (particularly in graphology, lexis, sentence

structure, and tenor) have been used to reflect the differing lifestyles and backgrounds of each target audience?

3 On your own, choose one of your texts and rewrite it for another specific target audience. Write an explanation of the changes you have made to the original.

Gotcha!

Any decent library will include a shelf full of books that explain the purposes and techniques of advertising. Space is too limited in this book to explain in detail but a few key points. Firstly, advertising aims to influence quite diverse audiences for many reasons:

■ to create market awareness about a product or service
■ to retain or increase a share in a market

- to reassure the trade/profession, staff and customers/clients about continuing quality
- to remain competitive and profitable by promoting brand/company image
- to make an appeal for financial aid or political support
- to make people spend their money, give to a cause, vote, take action of some kind.

Secondly, the methods that advertisers use are equally diverse, depending on their specific audience:

- offering a reward
  - material (a free gift)
  - moral (you will be a better mum by buying this toothpaste)
  - pure fantasy (men will notice you if you wear this perfume)
- appealing to basic emotions
  - guilt (your children will suffer if you don't buy this toothpaste)
  - fear (you will smell without this deodorant)
  - pride, envy or vanity
- confirming or altering attitudes (smoking v. non-smoking)
- reinforcing values (you are wise to invest in a private pension)
- appealing to any positive characteristics shared by groups or personality types.

Adverts don't just persuade in a broad sense; they also intrigue, inform, warn, advise, amuse and flatter. They engage your emotions.

But to work they must be noticed – and quickly, before you walk by, turn the page, or switch channels. To succeed, then, the advertisement writer (called the copywriter) must achieve five interrelated goals. Here is the Five Stage Plan:

Grab	**A**TTENTION
Arouse	**I**NTEREST
Create	**D**ESIRE
Give	**C**ONVICTION
Stimulate	**A**CTION

The copywriter will use a variety of linguistic, visual and auditory techniques to achieve these five points. Using the knowledge and skills you have been acquiring, you will now examine some of these techniques more closely.

The following texts are the opening portions of two lengthy ads. The first appeared in *Old Moore's Almanack*, an annual publication for persons interested in astrology and the paranormal; the second appeared in the financial supplement of the *Mail on Sunday*.

TEXT 65

'In the beginning was the Word, and the Word was God'
The Secret of the Ages Revealed
THE LOST WORD OF POWER PREVIOUSLY HIDDEN; KNOWN ONLY TO ADEPTS

The purchaser of this monograph is cautioned not to divulge it to others. It is the one, supreme Word. It is easy to pronounce. It cannot be revealed here. Within it is the heartbeat of the Cosmos. How to use the Word is revealed in THE LOST WORD OF POWER, a 4-page monograph by Frater E.L. Francis. The word is made up of only four letters and can be spoken anywhere and at any time you need it. We first published this monograph in 1985. Readers reported 'miracles'. One man wrote 'The effects are beyond anything I could possibly imagine…. It is worth more than all the money in the world'. Another man, who had failed with visualisation, rituals, etc, wrote: 'With THE LOST WORD I actually got aid when I needed it. I'm *still* getting it.' (Photocopies of these actual testimonials available on request.)

TEXT 66

THE LAZY MAN'S WAY TO A MILLION!!

Accountant confirms income of £7,000 a month!

DOES THE THOUGHT OF MAKING UP TO £7,000 A MONTH SOUND LIKE A GOOD IDEA?

Could you use an extra £84,000 over the next twelve months? Are you willing to work a few hours a week to achieve real wealth this year?

If you answered 'yes' to any of these questions, then I'm certain that you will want to learn more about my incredibly powerful GUARANTEED method of making over £1,500 net profit a week – every week – right from your own home.

This kind of income can be easily made without giving up your present job, or taking high risks with any of your hard earned money.

You'll be able to start this business immediately – and your profits can be rolling in within days.

But first, let me tell you a little more about myself, so you can see just how easy this business really is.

ACTIVITY 83

1 In groups, analyse both texts to discover how they use language to influence the target audience. Examine the graphology, lexis and semantic fields, grammar, and register.

2 How do the texts use the first four parts of the Five Stage Plan? Discuss to what extent these stages can be separated.

3 Draw up a detailed audience profile for each text. How is language used to engage with each audience? What makes each text acceptable to them?

Tricks of the trade

Throughout this book you have been raising your awareness of how language is selected and presented by writers for specific purposes and audiences. Copywriters themselves use dozens of linguistic and visual tricks to achieve their ends. As a critical student of language, you should not, however, underestimate your ability to detect and describe these tricks, even though you may not know the appropriate technical terms. Jargon is extremely useful for detailed analysis, but more important still is that you become sensitive to the ways in which writers use language.

You will have noticed that Texts 65 and 66 display a common aspect of ads – the repetition of the message in various ways. In addition, Text 66 addresses the reader early on by a series of questions, another standard technique. However, these particular questions deserve attention. Though they involve the audience, they are odd in that they don't *need* answering. The answer to each is assumed to be known already by both writer and audience. Then why ask the questions? Many reasons: to attract attention, to provoke thought, to reinforce an idea, and so on. The usefulness of this particular device of rhetoric explains its name: the **rhetorical question**.

The rhetorical question occurs in many types of text. Like so many other language devices it has been borrowed by copywriters to achieve particular effects. Though ads frequently use repetition as a device, they also employ many ways of compressing information, and in this they share much in common with, for instance, writers of poetry or of the headline and first paragraph of a newspaper report. It's easy to see how copywriters, sharing similar problems with other writers, have looked to those other genres and sub-genres for solutions.

You should therefore expect ads to:

- play around with graphology in their use of fonts, layout and punctuation
- exploit phonology in rhyme, rhythm and alliteration
- break up the structure of sentences
- rely heavily on the connotations of words
- play with words by altering spelling ('Kwik-Fit'), or by suggesting two or more meanings simultaneously (called a **pun** – 'There's a terrific *draught* in here', for a beer ad)
- create completely new words ('catisfaction' describing a cat food).

Many of these linguistic tricks or devices are called **figures of speech** in the criticism of literature. They share one fundamental characteristic: they are all unusual or unconventional ways of using language to foreground meaning.

Modifying the product

In Chapter 7 you looked at the way in which nouns in newspaper reports were described or 'modified' by a concentration of other words. To describe their products or services, advertisers use a number of common modifiers, mainly adjectives, such as 'new', 'improved', 'fresh', 'extra', 'better', 'real' and 'free'. They are often scattered repetitively throughout the text, and are usually more impressionistic than genuinely informative.

ACTIVITY 84

1 In groups of two or three, as a project, choose a specific product or service (perhaps shampoo, soap powder, or beer; banking, health insurance or expensive restaurants) and collect examples of ads from magazines, papers, television, packaging, leaflets, billboards.

2 Analyse your examples, and identify any similarities or marked differences in approach to the target audience. List the ten most commonly recurring modifiers. Are any related specifically to the product or service, or are they vague and impressionistic words?

3 Review your collection and locate examples of foregrounding in the graphology, phonology, grammar and lexis. Does any particular feature recur often? Can you relate this to the expectations of the target audience?

Choose a specific product (such as female or male perfume, car, chocolate bar, soft drink) and collect as many brand names as you can. What semantic fields and connotations do the names share in common? How are the various connotations connected, and why would the target audience find them acceptable? Write up your findings in the form of a report.

All the people some of the time

One idea that you've constantly kept in mind while examining a variety of texts is that of acceptability. It's time to inspect this a little more closely – and critically. In Chapter 6 you saw that magazines, even the more specialist, contain quite a variety of texts. Not all of these will appeal equally to members of the target audience, so the editor has to find the best compromise between satisfying readers and maintaining sales. The same is true of newspapers. The target audience of any publication can usually be subdivided into smaller (but overlapping) sections. In fact, the way that columns of classified ads in publications are organised (or 'classified') under separate subjects, clearly shows that readers do have many needs and interests. Few readers read *everything*.

The ideal reader, imagined and created by the publication for each section, reads in perfect acceptance of the text. You, as a real reader, may not. You will not be so informed about or interested in some items, you won't share quite the same values or ideas; you won't therefore quite fit the profile for the target audience of these items or of the related ads. This ideal representative of the target audience is often referred to as the **implied reader**, and your relationship to it is worth questioning. And to do that you will examine a short ad.

TEXT 67
PRODUCT RECALL

Due to the alarming number of incidents of sexual harassment of men, we have decided to withdraw batch 4379-4381. Lynx apologises to any men who have had their bottoms pinched or have experienced women making overly suggestive comments. However, if this kind of behaviour does not bother you, feel free to hold on to your can.
THE LYNX EFFECT

This ad (full-page and including a photograph of the product), appeared in *FHM*, a magazine aimed at young males sharing interests in sex, fashion, mainstream sports, pop culture, and more sex.

1   In small groups, identify the values and beliefs that the magazine assumes are held by the implied reader of this text. List as many separate aspects as possible in order to construct a detailed profile of this ideal.

Only when you have completed this first activity should you read the observations at the end of this chapter. Then continue with:

2   In larger groups, compare and discuss your profiles. How does the ad attempt to persuade real readers that they should adopt the values you have uncovered, or reinforce their existing beliefs? Examine both the general method and approach as well as specific linguistic techniques.

3   To what particular cultural myth would you relate your findings? How easy is it for readers to recognise or seriously question assumptions made about the target audience?

Take your positions!

In discussing biography, Chapter 4 introduced the idea that a writer can 'position the reader' (referring, of course, to the ideal implied reader). In other words, a writer can use language in ways that cause the reader to adopt unconsciously and uncritically a particular position. One way is by choice of pronoun either to suggest the viewpoint of the narrator or to directly address the reader. More subtle ways include the degree of shared knowledge and values that a writer assumes the reader to possess. The reader is 'positioned' in relation to the text, seduced into accepting the assumptions and implications contained within it.

If you as a reader find the text acceptable, then the writer has succeeded in capturing your attention. You will read and interpret the text in the way intended by the writer, a way often referred to as the 'preferred' or 'dominant' reading. In other words, preferred and accepted by the majority of readers. But some readers don't accept certain texts; they will resist or reject them. And if they find too many such texts in a magazine they will stop buying it. Much of the earlier discussion of Text 63 revolved around the target audience and the ways in which the writer constructed the text to make it acceptable to them. No doubt many readers accepted the dominant reading, but some others would have rejected it as being too idealistic, too reliant on out-of-date stereotypes, as being patronising or insulting to women and their roles in today's society. Of course, any particular publication believes that the vast majority of its readers will accept a text, and that those who don't will nevertheless accept most of the others.

Ads are handy everyday texts for making important points about critical reading. You have examined a fairly straightforward example by a copywriter to promote a product for personal hygiene, but the concept of positioning the reader applies equally to other genres.

ACTIVITY 87

Take another look at Text 14 on p 15. In two or three paragraphs, explain how the text attempts to position the reader into accepting a particular view of events.

New improved?

Examining ads for the same type of product over a period of time can give an insight into the way that the copywriter targets his audience. Here are three ads for fairly similar products, aimed primarily at adult women.

TEXT 68 (pub 1886)

A LOVELY COMPLEXION and beautiful soft and fair neck, hands, and arms can only be obtained by the daily use of **ROWLANDS' KALYDOR**, a most cooling, soothing, healing, and refreshing preparation for the Skin and Complexion of Ladies, and all exposed to the summer sun and dust; it effectually eradicates all Freckles, Tan, Sunburn, Stings of Insects, Prickly Heat, Cutaneous Eruptions, Roughness and Redness of the

Skin, Pimples, &c.; cures Inflammation, Burns, Erysipelas, Excema, Inflamed Eyes, &c., and produces a beautifully pure and delicate complexion; it has for more than sixty years been known as the only safe and reliable preparation for healing and soothing the skin of the most delicate lady or child, and is warranted perfectly free from any lead, poisonous, or metallic ingredients, or oxide of zinc, of which most skin cosmetics are composed, and which ruin the complexion. Soaps which are not allowed to remain on the skin cannot possibly have any healing or beautifying effect on it – therefore, avoid cheap soaps and greasy cosmetics, and try only **ROWLANDS' KALYDOR**, of 20, HATTON GARDEN, LONDON, and beware of cheap spurious imitations under the same or similar names. Sold everywhere. Half-Pint Bottles, 4s. 6d.; Quarter-Pint Bottles, 2s. 3d.; Pints, 8s. 6d.

TEXT 69 (pub 1926)
LETTERS OF A DÉBUTANTE

MAYFAIR, *Tuesday*
Dear Freda

I have made Lady Sylvia my friend for life! You know that unfortunate complexion of hers – all rough, poor girl, and so dreadfully sensitive? Well, I've been taking her in hand with my precious Icilma Cream, and you wouldn't believe *the difference it's made to her! The soothing touch of the Algerian Beauty-water on it has just the protection her skin needed – she looks quite lovely now – all delicate and velvety like a peach.*

We were riding in the Row this morning – a beautiful day, but oh! the wind and dust! Captain Egerton came along and positively burst into song about 'Pretty maids all in the Row.' I fancy Lady Sylvia values that young man's opinion – and shall be interested to watch developments!

I've just got one of the new Icilma Poudre Compactes – the most dinky thing you ever saw. Icilma for ever!

Yours light-heartedly

Gwenda

Icilma

THE CREAM OF SOCIETY

1/3 per jar. Large size 2/-. Vanity Bag size 9d. In beautiful jade-coloured jars. Two perfumes – Bouquet, Blue Carton, Red Seals, or Magnolia, Green Carton, Green Seals. Please ask for the perfume you require. Icilma Face Powder, two tints, Naturelle and Creme, 1/3 per box.

TEXT 70 (pub 1993)
NEW
Protection For Today's Environment

In today's changing environment, we face new aggressive elements: air pollution, central heating, air conditioning, artificial and natural light. The skin becomes dull, dehydrated and sensitive.
Clarins responds with
MOISTURE LOTION HYDRATION-PLUS
An exceptionally light, fluid day lotion with moisturizing and soothing properties. Offers complete skin comfort and protection. Concentrated with natural plant extracts and vitamins proven to soften fine lines and promote a glowing healthy looking skin. Quick and easy to use, ideal for all skin types and all ages.
Discover the unique benefits for yourself. Come and visit the Clarins Specialist today and receive your complimentary sample of Moisture Lotion Hydration-Plus.
THE SPECIALIST IN SKIN AND HAIR
CLARINS
-PARIS-

ACTIVITY 88

1 On your own, in preparation for a group workshop, analyse all three texts. In particular, look at the choices in lexis (including semantic fields, specialist vocabulary and connotations), grammar, and register. Record your analysis with examples.

2 In groups, compare your prepared analyses. Discuss and agree your assessment of the register of each, bearing in mind that the target audience for each is different in *time* What difficulties are there in appreciating the intended effect of each ad?

3 Nominate one person from the group to draw up a list of agreed similarities and differences. Discuss how fundamental are the similarities between the ads. What sort of appeal is made to each target audience?

The differences between the ads should not mislead you into thinking that each subsequent ad is a new improved version of the previous one. You can assume that each ad was written by an experienced copywriter, fully aware of appropriate techniques and of the audience targeted. Some of the differences suggest that the product meant something different in the lives of each audience.

ACTIVITY 89

1 In groups, from the evidence in Texts 68, 69 and 70, discuss how you think each audience would have perceived the product.

2 Text 70 appeared in *New Woman*, a

magazine aimed at independent young women. How does the copywriter use language in this ad to position the reader?

I'm sorry, I'll read that again

Here are two very different texts that nevertheless share some interesting features.

TEXT 71

Are you happy with the coffee you buy? Maybe you shouldn't be.

[here appeared a photograph of a Brazilian woman behind a barcode, as if in prison]

She works on a Brazilian coffee plantation from 5am to darkness.

She and her children are paid just £1 a day. Between them.

She's exploited by a trading system controlled by people in another continent.

She needs you to realize you're part of this system.

She needs you to persuade your supermarket to stock coffee that gives workers a living wage.

Fill in the coupon and we'll show you how your consumer power can do this.

Please send me details of how I can help Third World workers achieve a better life. Also a list of people-friendly products already on sale.

Name _____ Address _____

_____

_____ Postcode _____   **Christian Aid**

To: Christian Aid, Freepost, London SE1 7YY or call 0839 200 100 for more information. **We believe in life before death**

TEXT 72

My secret affair

Last December we moved to a new house. Our milkman was very kind and helpful, making us feel most welcome. One day I invited him in, and we sat on the couch in the living room. Well ... one thing led to another, and before we knew it, that other thing led to something else. It's now been going on for over three months. Then last Thursday, as he was quietly leaving the house, the gate suddenly fell off its hinges, causing a terrific noise. All the neighbours heard the commotion and I'm sure the rumours are spreading already. What should I do?

Jayne.

Well Jayne, there are two things you can do: either replace the old gate (any good local DIY store will have an extensive range of wood or wrought iron designs). Or why not try a lick of new paint? It's amazing how something old can be given a new lease of life. Or there again, try a cup of 99 tea. It won't do your gate much good, but who cares anyway!

ACTIVITY 90

1 In small groups, examine Text 71 to discover the ways that language is used to affect its audience. Pay particular attention to grammar (sentence type and structure, active and passive voice, pronoun use), lexis (denotation & connotation), and graphology. How does this appeal fulfil the Five Stage Plan?

2 What are the writer's purposes? How does the writer position the reader in order to achieve them?

Both texts were published in general magazines, the *Radio Times* and *TV Times* respectively. Both took up a full page. In its complete form Text 72 appeared with three other 'letters' as an Agony Aunt column entitled 'Heart to Heart', below which was a seemingly unconnected brief ad for 99 Tea.

ACTIVITY 91

1 In small groups, discuss the likely reaction of the target audience to Text 72. Why was the ad composed in this format?

2 What similarities do both texts display in terms of approach to target audience? Do you think their unconventional aspects make them more effective? What genre does Text 72 belong to? Why?

COMMENTARY

In examining Texts 71 and 72, you will have noticed that both initially mislead the reader. In each case the reader's expectations, given the context of the magazine and the format of the text, would lead them to believe they were reading a coffee ad and a problem page. In the case of Text 71 the subsequent realisation reinforces the challenging nature of the appeal; in the case of Text 72 the humour increases the ad's effectiveness.

However, at a slightly deeper level, this similarity reveals much more about the nature of texts. Text 71 is deliberately constructed in an ambiguous way; at first only one interpretation (that it is a coffee ad) is apparent. When the penny drops that it's an appeal, the real interpretation becomes clear, and the ambiguity becomes apparent. The close relationship between product ads and appeals is used to enhance the effect of the Christian Aid text. In other words, intertextuality between the text-types has been exploited.

Text 72 is a more extreme case. Here, the sub-genre of the problem page, something normally far removed from the advertising world, is borrowed to amuse and to sell. It is a problem page only in format and superficial content; it is actually a parody and an ad. It works by relying on your knowledge of other types of text – your appreciation of intertextuality – and it plays around with them.

Review

This book could easily have begun by looking at ads. After all, they are familiar to all of us and don't seem to pose any threat. But they've been left till now deliberately. In other chapters you've discovered and practised a range of analytical skills. These have allowed you to go beyond the merely superficial so that you engage more critically with the purposes and assumptions of writers, not only of ads but of all types of text.

Within this book you have seen a number of texts that make use of the letter format: Texts 12 and 13 in Chapter 1, Text 40 in Chapter 5, Texts 50–53 in Chapter 6, and Texts 69 and 72 in this present chapter. As a format it is obviously versatile, effective and multi-functional. But advertisers borrow such formats to exploit them. They rely on the reader's intertextual knowledge of the more usual and expected contexts for these formats. Text 67, for instance, relies intertextually on your knowledge that manufacturers sometimes publish warning notices in appropriate publications to recall faulty goods. In fact, though you can talk about the language of the law or of religion, of chemistry or of criminology, you cannot in the same way talk about the language of advertising. Because there isn't one.

To exist, advertising must borrow from other subjects, other formats, and other genres and sub-genres. It uses techniques of language taken from the registers of other occupations and social situations. Like a chameleon it changes its appearance to suit its surrounding audience. And that's why this chapter title describes ads as 'Eclectic'. If you are 'eclectic', you borrow from the best of a variety of styles, methods, or ideas. That's what ads do.

In Chapter 2 you saw that the boundaries between genres are far from clear, and that in fact genres borrow from one another and so constantly evolve. How, then, can advertising be classified if not by format, sub-genre or even genre? The answer is by **discourse**. If you study other aspects of language, you will sooner or later come across this term, which now has a number of rather different meanings depending on its particular context. It's therefore worth trying to prevent possible confusion by ending with a brief note on some of these.

Discourse

Discourse used to refer only to spontaneous spoken language, and in the term 'discourse analysis' it very often preserves this meaning. It can also function as a synonym for what is commonly referred to as a 'text': any stretch of language, spoken, written or electronically recorded. But in a much broader way it can refer to the whole body of facts, ideas, beliefs and opinions that make up a subject. So, for instance, you can speak of the discourse of politics or the discourse of medicine. In this last sense, a discourse is likely to make use of several genres or formats. The discourse of politics involves communication through speech, debate, party political broadcast, interview, white paper, poster, pamphlet, report, memoir, textbook, and so on. The medium and format may vary, but all contain a common store of knowledge and ideology, and a common core of language use.

Finally, then, discourse can include both the texts through which communication takes place, and the contexts in which the interaction between writer (or speaker) and audience occurs. Don't worry too much if at first this seems a bit difficult to grasp. The fact of the matter is that throughout this book you have been engaged in analysing the discourse of subjects. In other words, you haven't just been studying texts as collections of words and sentences that have no meaning or existence outside of the page, you have been analysing and interpreting them as part of a real world in which motivated people produce texts to influence other people. It therefore makes sense to speak of the discourse of advertising – a topic that potentially is completely open-ended in its borrowing of topic, genre, register and style of language as the need arises.

In this chapter you have examined some of the many techniques that the copywriter uses to manipulate an audience. You have also attended more closely to the ways in which the copywriter chooses language to represent assumptions made about that audience. Your skills of analysis and criticism should now be considerably developed.

COMMENTARY
On Text 63

- The content largely concerns a family day out; facts about the car are 'slipped in' at intervals, as if less important.
- Semantic fields of motor cars ('five gears', '1.3 litres', 'top speed') and family day out ('towels, buckets, spades', 'Sand between toes') are fairly obvious. More specifically, there are also semantic fields of space/comfort ('wonderfully relaxed', 'welcoming comfort', 'Plenty of room', 'snuggle down') and freedom/escape ('No thought given', 'Caution thrown to the wind', 'as we speed'). Both serve to link the car with the excursion.
- Jargon of motor cars ranges only from semi-technical ('1.3 litres', 'halogen headlights') to the most general ('room in the back', 'the stereo').
- Though the description of separate 'holiday' events is sparse, the cumulative effect of their connotations is to suggest a certain type of holiday – one that is basically cheap and cheerful. It is family focused

('buckets, spades and children', 'Ice-cream', 'Prince catching John out').
Socially it implies a lower class family that can afford only a small car, a
family that eats at a 'roadside cafe' (not 'café,'), drinks tea from 'mugs'
(not cups), and enjoys 'The works all round'. It is also a very English
holiday ('Bacon and eggs', 'Cricket', 'Scones and jam').

- With two exceptions the sentences are not grammatically complete.
  Many appear to be sentences only because they begin with a capital
  letter and end with a full stop. This aspect is further discussed on pages
  95–96.
- Reference is either to 'I/my' or 'we/our', the latter including family.
- The text comprises one paragraph that recounts a family outing from
  morning to evening.
- The appearance of the one paragraph is made more reader-friendly by
  the wide spacing between the lines and the upper-case lettering of the
  first word in each sentence. (In fact, this second device seems to provide
  a structural cohesion that would otherwise be missing through the
  unconventional sentence structure).
- The title acts in much the same way as a newspaper headline. It
  summarises the contents of the following paragraph: a list of 'my'
  favourite family 'things'. Being also a line from an old popular song, it is
  linked culturally to the target audience; it contains alliteration ('few' and
  'Favorit') as well as a deviant (deliberately altered) spelling that
  foregrounds a play on words between 'favourite' and the car model
  name.

The above points go some way to answering the earlier activity questions,
but they don't yet fully explain the ad's format and purpose. In other
words: why was it written in this particular way?

In terms of content, not only is the lifestyle of the family very English and
classbound, it is also highly idealised. No mishaps occur: family life appears
blissful and childhood in particular is a happy, fun-filled time. The ad
portrays what is called a **cultural myth**, in other words a set of beliefs or
attitudes that a culture shares about a subject. Cultural myths are simplified
and idealised: think, for example, about the dominant beliefs surrounding
the countryside/city relationship and the Green movement, or about the
roles of males and females in society. This particular ad exploits shared
beliefs about how families are expected to behave, and it does this by a
careful selection of lexis that will trigger off the appropriate connotations in
the minds of the target audience.

The text itself is impressionistic and evocative, related in a 'snap-shot' style
much as you might record such a day in a photo album or diary. It's also a
list of highlights, in some ways reminiscent of the way you might let your
mind wander over the day just gone (a technique called **stream of
consciousness** in the analysis of fiction). Certainly the lexis and the lack of
formal sentence structure indicate the intimate tone of someone revealing
domestic trivia about their family. The ad carefully avoids mentioning
adult gender, though a couple is implied in addition to children. However,
the 'voice' of the text strongly suggests a stereotypical mother who for a day
exchanges the cares of 'shopping or housework' for the pleasures of the

'golden sunset' and a 'walk arm-in-arm', but ends as always by 'tucking the children' up in bed. The lack of technical jargon about the car confirms this stereotype, as naturally she won't understand detailed specifications.

The car, then, can provide not just the day out, but also domestic joy and a perfect family lifestyle. The ad confirms the values shared by a section of society about family life and the desirability of material possessions. It also recreates particular emotions to suggest that these can be experienced by owning the product. It entertains by its abbreviated narrative structure, and it no doubt arouses nostalgic memories in the minds of many by its generalised references. And *in doing all of these things* it tries to persuade the target audience, the mother, that her family should buy the car. A popular general family magazine like the *Radio Times* is just the place for such an ad.

COMMENTARY

On Text 67

Some of the underlying values and beliefs you should have discovered in the text are:

1 Personal body odour is not acceptable and cannot be attractive.
2 Use of an anti-perspirant deodorant is essential to 'solve' your personal 'problem'.
3 There is such a thing as an aphrodisiac, and Lynx is an exceptionally potent one.
4 It is permissible for women to take the initiative in sexual matters.
5 It is also permissible for women to demonstrate their sexual interest from the outset in mildly aggressive ways.
6 Men will find points **4** & **5** enjoyable.
7 Heterosexual relations are the norm. (Note that homosexual behaviour is not explicitly excluded, but the mention of 'women' suggests the 'natural' relationship.)
8 Points **1** to **7** inclusive reflect 'normal' attitudes and behaviour.

Further reading:

Words In Ads by Greg Myers, Edward Arnold (1994). A comprehensive, lucid and most enjoyable introduction to the ways in which language is used in advertising.

The Discourse of Advertising by Guy Cook, Routledge (1992). A rather more demanding book, but one that you can dip into with confidence and profit after reading the first.

9 Texts About Texts

In this chapter you will examine some actual answers submitted by students on texts that you have seen earlier in this book. You will also improve your exam performance both by learning more active ways of reading and by applying your knowledge of textual criticism to your own writing.

In earlier chapters you have seen that many texts occur within larger texts, articles within magazines or newspapers for example. However, many texts are also written about other texts. Textbooks often serve to explain more difficult and complicated texts, while regular publications often contain reviews of books, articles, TV and radio programmes, etc. This professional writing about texts is not unlike the apprentice writing about texts that you are all too often asked to perform: the examination answer.

An example question

To begin, take another look at Text 62: 'The boy William did well'. In that chapter you were asked to write an answer to the question: 'How does the writer use language to influence the reader's view of the two political leaders?' You were also given some pointers on appropriate features (semantic fields, graphology and tenor), though you would be expected to discuss others that you saw as relevant. You should, of course, have attempted this question yourself before you read on.

The openings of answers are crucially important. They are the first point of contact with the examiner, and it's obviously in your own interests to make a suitably successful first impression. The examiner is hoping to find an opening paragraph displaying not only clarity of expression, but also a sense of purpose and direction that is likely to produce an organised response. From a scale of Poor, Average, Good, Very Good and Excellent, here are just three openings to the question: a poor one, a good, and a very good. Spelling and punctuation have been tidied up where necessary, but otherwise words are just as they were written under exam conditions. The examiner's comments are also included, referenced to the particular sections of the answers.

Poor

The first thing of note in this article is that it is politically based.[1] The first thing of note[2] is that the first paragraph is in a larger and bolder font, whereas the second is in a smaller less bold font, unlike the rest of the article which is even smaller.[3]

Also[4] this article is ridden with spoken language[5] which is shown with the use of speech marks, for example 'Tony'.[6] As well as a fair amount of asking questions.[7] However, largely speaking this piece appears to be written language due to its layout and use of punctuation.[8] I would most probably say that this article came from a broadsheet newspaper as the paragraphs are quite long and there isn't a huge emphasis on photographs.[9]

Examiner's Comments

[1] An awkward way of saying that the text is a political article.

[2] Second thing?

[3] Another awkwardly expressed observation; no comment offered on why this is 'of note'.

[4] No reason for new paragraph so soon. Lack of coherence becoming apparent in the separate topic of each sentence.

[5] Odd lexical choice of 'ridden' implies an unfavourable value judgement about the observation on spoken language.

[6] Weak example.

[7] Poor sentence structure expressing too vague a comment.

[8] Unclear what this further vague statement means.

[9] Identifying type of newspaper (wrongly) isn't helpful, while reasons are yet again too vague.

This student is confused from the very start of his answer. Apart from the weak expression, the actual content moves from some general comment on graphology through vague remarks on the inclusion of speech to the grand statement that the text is mainly written. A purely descriptive approach that provides no signposts for a detailed answer and doesn't actually begin to answer the question. A somewhat better opening was:

Good

The piece is typical of a tabloid newspaper piece in the way it is both written and presented.[1] The choice of words from the writer such as 'He was wetting his knickers' and 'the Commons playground' indicate the piece is very casual[2] and the writer is using sarcasm[3] in an attempt to get a laugh, as we know that the Commons is supposed to be a serious place and not a playground, although it may appear this way.[4]

The purpose of this piece is to report on the first day of Parliament and the confrontations between Tony Blair and William Hague.[5] The piece however sides heavily with Tony Blair, not particularly by singing his praises, but more by putting down William Hague.[6]

Examiner's Comments

[1] Student displays knowledge of sub-genre in a clear opening statement.

[2] Too specific too soon, especially as the next sentence reverts to more general introductory comment.

[3] Description arguably not bitter or scathing enough to warrant term 'sarcasm', but the word is now often used with diluted meaning.

[4] Sentence ends with more scene-setting comment, showing overall understanding of both the text and its context.

[5] Another basic but helpful statement which can be developed.

[6] Yes, though not at end of article. However, at this point student can be forgiven for not noticing this.

Here the student has early on tried to locate the text as typically tabloid, and supply linguistic evidence in support. He next identifies what he sees as the purpose of the text, although at this stage it is a simplistic statement. However, you can already detect the beginnings of an analytical and evaluative approach to the text, even if not fully under control.

Very good

The piece of text is a newspaper article concerning politics, more specifically about Question Time between Prime Minister Tony Blair and Opposition Leader William Hague.[1]
Despite being a serious subject the tone is quite informal, even colloquial and sensational.[2] For example the writer – Matthew Parris – uses the phrase 'He was wetting his knickers' as an idiom[3] to indicate how scared and nervous Hague was; also phrases such as 'William was scared' and 'sitting on the edge of his seat' give the text an exciting, sensational tone.[4] Other factors of the informality in the piece[5] include calling the two important politicians by their first names – 'Tony' and 'William' – which has the effect of bringing them on the level with the reader, as someone they might meet and speak to in the street.[6]

Examiner's Comments

[1] Clear and concise identification of text source and content.

[2] Aspect of tenor chosen for immediate analysis and accurately summarised, but a pity no indication given of other aspects to be discussed.

[3] Use of appropriate specific terminology – good.

[4] Examples provided from several parts of text to support assertions made.

[5] Rather awkward phrasing.

[6] Further examples of a different nature (mode of address) develop initial comment on tone.

Admittedly the phrasing could occasionally be improved, but after quickly identifying the topic, this student concentrates upon one significant aspect. She makes an assertion about tone, provides appropriate and varied textual examples as evidence, and adds further explanation and comment to expand upon the initial assertion. This was well developed in the subsequent paragraph, not reproduced here. The first paragraph is exceptionally short, but the subsequent change of topic and focus explains its isolation. An excellent answer would have provided an outline of its proposed shape and organisation before discussing one aspect in such detail.

Reading to write

Whether you are preparing a text in the classroom, at home or in the exam hall, you can save precious time by following a few simple principles. Some of these involve the way you first read the text. In Chapter 2 you were reminded of three elementary stages in reading that form the basis for developing critical skills. As you become practised you can very often perform all three stages simultaneously, depending on the difficulty of the particular text. However, there is a further crucial distinction to make between what can be called active as opposed to passive reading.

You engage in passive reading essentially to pass the time: reading a magazine in a dentist's waiting room, a billboard on the way home, the daily paper, some junk mail, a book by your bed at night. Throughout this book you have been learning to read more actively, in other words critically. You should have a number of questions in your mind about each text, and you should be actively searching for the answers. The framework for analysis gives you the basic set of questions that open up a 'way in' to the text; you then go on to develop these questions according to the type of text you are examining.

It's essential that you make the best possible use of the time available to you, and this is especially true in the exam situation. Sadly, you haven't time for the luxury of reading the text for enjoyment (wait till after the exam); you need to read it actively from the word go. You should therefore *always* read a text with pen in hand, marking things that strike you *as you read*. It is a disheartening experience to find, after reading a text from start to finish, that you've nothing to show for it but the same bare text staring back up at you. You must therefore *always* read with the purpose of answering questions that you are asking yourself, and you note those answers in your own personalised shorthand (described below) on the text.

How exactly does this work? You will first have read the question and identified the key words within it.

Text reading 1

You read the text to understand the content and writer's attitude, as well as to link it to the demands of the examiner's question. You mark the text as things strike you (unusual lexis, excessive punctuation or changes of font, in fact *anything* that seems to be foregrounded in a striking manner, or that seems worth noting).

Text reading 2

Now that you've got the measure of the text, you read it again in a careful and more systematic way. You are looking for the key examples of features and aspects relevant to the question, and you mark or note them on the text. You find them by constantly asking questions, taking your framework for analysis as your starting point.

Text reading 3

You read once more to check that you have collected basic textual evidence for each aspect of the examiner's question, and that you haven't overlooked or misinterpreted anything.

What are the advantages of this approach?

1 It forces you to take the time necessary to collect and organise your thoughts before you begin to write.
2 It forces you to answer a question by the best possible method: asking and answering related questions that you are already familiar with.
3 Your annotations represent a number of 'signposts' that will act both to point to key features and to provide the valuable evidence for them.
4 Following a regular tried and tested procedure will give you confidence in your own ability.

As a working example, what did the 'Very Good' candidate mark on her copy of the text, before she began to write? The actual question had pointed her towards semantic fields, graphology and tenor, all of which she had underlined. Using the simple abbreviations of 'SF', 'G' and 'T' she had written these against selected items in the text, with occasional words of explanation. For example, against the strapline 'Blair versus Hague: Round One' she had written 'G–SF (boxing)'; against 'wetting his knickers': 'T–SF (childhood)'; against the repeated section of 'Tony said he hadn't, William said he had': 'G–T– SF (child)'. She had also ringed some key words and phrases: 'Tony', 'gang', 'Commons playground', 'Hague's mum', 'Prime Minister' and 'Premier'. These were enough to provide not only some important examples, but also to establish links between the three features.

With each text you read, you should therefore aim to develop your own personal way of annotating texts – your own shorthand. You might, for instance, use 'Gr' for grammar and 'Gph' for graphology; you might underline words from key semantic fields, ring figures of speech, double underline key quotations; you could also use a colour coding scheme (not too arty!), and so on. By these means you will develop a quick and powerful method of breaking down a text into its component parts as well as highlighting the crucial textual evidence that you will need for your answer. After your final careful reading you are ready to organise your proposed answer in your opening paragraph. Your annotated text shows you the plan for your answer, and you write this up for the examiner accordingly. The examiner, on the other hand, will subsequently read your first paragraph to discover the structure of your answer: the signposts you will be using for the direction and order of your ideas.

ACTIVITY 92

1 Re-read the opening paragraph of your answer to the Blair/Hague text as if you were an examiner. Does it summarise the text by stating its topic and main purpose? Does it indicate the structure of the following sections?

2 Re-write your opening paragraph in no more than four sentences so that it provides a full and clear introduction to your answer.

The full monty

Next you will examine a complete answer to a question. Not a perfect one nor a bad one, but one that demonstrates some important features of the exam answer. Chapter 7 included a tabloid article on Ruth Ellis (Text 61), followed by a detailed activity. Your examination of the text there revolved around the general question 'Identify the ways in which language is used effectively in this text'. You discussed the text in groups.

ACTIVITY 102

Now, individually, tackle the above question and write your answer as if in an exam. Allow yourself no more than an hour, and use the reading technique outlined earlier.

Here is a student's response, written under exam conditions in one hour.

The writer's attitude to capital punishment is very clear throughout the text.[1] His article, titled 'The woman who hangs today' has many explicit references to the subject of hanging.[2] He describes it as 'dreadful', 'obscene', 'fierce', sickening' and 'barbarous'.[3] However,[4] throughout the article he fails to mention anything of the crime committed by Ruth Ellis other than that she was a 'murderess'. This proves[5] that to him, hanging is unjustifiable, regardless of the crime. It is simply another murder: 'disobeying the sixth commandment which says "Thou shalt not kill"'.[6]

The article, written about the last female to be hanged,[7] is by no means a debate article but is overflowing with loaded, emotive words, which vividly express the writer's opinion.[8] He describes the executioner as 'wretched', hanging as 'atrocious affairs' and the public will as 'savage'.[9]

By using a number of techniques[10] in order to convey his opinion, he succeeds in making the article very manipulative.[11] Throughout the article he refers to the time of the hanging 'If you read this at nine o'clock', thus making the event true to life, more personal and not just another news article. These statements are in larger capital letters for emphasis and effect, and he reinforces this point with the use of pronouns giving the impression that we were somehow involved in it.[12]

Reading on it becomes apparent that he wants the reader to feel somehow connected with it in order to experience the guilt: 'the guilt ... will belong to us', 'the dregs of shame'. According to him, we are all responsible for Ruth Ellis' unjustifiable hanging simply by being members of society. [13]

A surprisingly small amount of quotes are used within the article yet those in it are carefully selected and effective.[14] By using quotes he not only separates certain comments from his opinion but he succeeds in making these particularly horrific statements stand out: 'some vantage point', 'to form an impression of the physique of the prisoner'.

This description of how the prisoner is watched before the hanging gives the act an element of secrecy and deception.[15] At the beginning of the text the reader is told that the hangman 'will have been slipped into the prison'. However, if everyone approved of hanging why would such secrecy be needed?[16] By including such statements, the writer is commenting on how controversial and even old-fashioned hanging is. Words such as 'executioner' and 'medieval' convey a historical picture [17]

Another element that is present in the article is sarcasm. He begins by saying 'It's a fine day for haymaking. A fine day for fishing', then 'it's a fine day for a hanging'. At the very end of the article, after giving a horrific account of a hanging, he again says 'Yes, it is a fine day'. Despite only being short, this is a very dramatic statement.[18] He realises that many people, including politicians, are against hanging but continue to turn a blind eye to it.

Although the article is full of powerful words, the writer has included purely objective but horrific statements where the facts speak for themselves: 'the body will be left to hang for one hour'. There is no imagery in the statement yet it creates a vivid almost sick picture.[19]

It is obvious from the article that the writer believes his opinion, despite being controversial, to be right. He writes with such confidence and manipulation, ending the piece[20] with the dramatic paragraph: 'I am a sucker for all human faces because I hope I am a sucker for all humanity, good or bad. But I prefer the face not to be lolling because of a judicially broken neck'. [21]

Examiner's comments:

[1] Opening sentence is positive and assured, suggesting that student has read the text attentively. She also indicates that her approach to effective language use will focus on the writer's communication of his attitude.

[2] No further outline or 'signposts' for future direction of answer; instead she begins to develop the idea contained in first sentence.

[3] Good selection of relevant quotations, appropriately punctuated, to clarify assertion about writer's attitude.

[4] Good link, signalling that an important contrast is about to follow.

[5] No, it may suggest a point of view but it doesn't prove it.

[6] An appropriate quote to support previous sentence, though a little too long.

[7] No need to repeat information supplied by examiner. This second paragraph is too short and similar in content for it to be separated from the first.

[8] Reinforces one-sided nature of text.

[9] Attempts to broaden aspects of writer's attitude, with further textual evidence. Student ranges over the text well for quotes.

[10] Good 'signpost' that a linked series of features will be discussed.

[11] Yes, but 'manipulative' will need more explanation.

[12] Three good points. Each could do with a little more detail, but audience involvement is stressed.

[13] Emotional appeal explained, with two good quotes, and links are made with earlier comments; *writer's* attitude stressed. Excellent paragraph, but would be better organised as conclusion of previous one.

[14] Another good observation, followed by explanation and evidence.

[15] Further observation, linked to preceding paragraph.

[16] Rhetorical question adds variety to prose style.

[17] Again, textual evidence for comment is given. Picture is 'archaic' rather than simply 'historical'.

[18] Well observed, though this is irony, not sarcasm.

[19] Student has noticed late on that some descriptions rely on their effect by being factual and denotative. Therefore adds this paragraph.

[20] No – it's not the last paragraph.

[21] *Not* a satisfactory final paragraph. It's a vague summary followed by an excessively long quote, and though it does summarise the writer's attitude well, it doesn't summarise 'the ways in which language is used' or draw conclusions about how 'effective' they are.

Examiner's summary:

A pity that the student didn't write a little more, though her time reading and annotating the text was patently well spent. The opening statement clearly indicates her intended approach, and leads to an organised and highly cohesive central part. In addition she regularly provides textual evidence for her assertions, together with frequent comment or explanation. Occasionally a quotation is overlong. Quotations should be no more than five or six words; any necessary longer quotes should be referred to by the line numbers that examiners thoughtfully provide. Some phrasing is a little awkward, some points are insufficiently developed, and there is a general lack of specific terminology, but these weaknesses are very much compensated by the student's obvious *sensitivity to language*. The lack of an appropriate conclusion – ran out of time? – sadly spoils this otherwise very good response.

Thankfully, examiners are sufficiently human not to expect perfection. Wherever possible they seek to reward you for what you have achieved, not penalise you for what you haven't. They are only too well aware of the difficulties and pressures of the exam hall.

Now you see it!

The following is in some respects a more difficult text, but don't be put off by this. It's the opening of a lecture explaining her need for self-expression given by the writer and journalist Anaïs Nin. (Note: The reference to *Werther* in the first paragraph is to a highly popular novel published in the eighteenth century by the German writer Goethe. Many young German romantics of the time copied the fate of the hero by committing suicide themselves.)

TEXT 73

The Artist as Magician

Sooner or later a magician is always asked the source of the magic which he practices. By what formulas, what words, what means did I acquire not only a sense of magic about life that nothing could destroy but also how was I able to impart it? How was it that when Goethe's *Werther* was published there was a rash of suicides, whereas when my diaries came out there was a rash of anti-suicides? How did all this happen?

I remember that as children we were very unhappy because of great dissension between the parents. My father was a pianist and my mother was a singer. The quarrels would overwhelm and frighten us. But then suddenly there would be a quiet time. The piano would begin, my mother would begin to sing, and there would be peace again. And there would be great joy in the house, and the children felt free and they began to dance. This became for me a symbol and established a tremendous indebtedness and love for what I call the art spirits which we are celebrating today. That no matter what the human condition, no matter what kinds of infernos and destructive wars our dictators plunged us into, there was always this escape, this power to transfigure, transform, and transmute.

I learned from this that in order to resist the sorrows of human experience we needed another world. Unfortunately our culture kept calling that world an escape, making it a most unvirtuous thing to do, to escape from the present. To escape from everything was really not taking part and not being involved in life. I don't understand how it happened but it was part of our ideology, and there was a great taboo on anybody who was able to move away from catastrophe. It wasn't realized that the moving away from catastrophe or trauma or ugliness or whatever monsters we encounter was *necessary* as an *anti-toxin*. We need anti-toxins, we need a place in which to recover our vision, we need a place in which to reconstruct ourselves after shattering experiences. I discovered that very early, and my magic was simply the power to move away from paralyzing, destructive experience.

ACTIVITY 94

Write an answer to the question below. You can choose whether you do this as a timed piece in one hour, or as an untimed assignment. Either way, you should now possess the skill and confidence to make a number of observations and critical comments that describe, explain and evaluate the particular stylistic fingerprints of this writer and speaker. Consequently, no observations for the text need appear at the end of this chapter. Good luck!

'Identify and describe some of the distinctive features of language in the text, and assess their effectiveness. In your answer you should include comment on lexis, grammar, figures of speech, register, and audience.'

Further reading:

Two books that will help you further develop your analytical skills are:

Cohesion in English by M Halliday & R Hasan, Longman (1976). A lengthy book, so try Chapter 7 for a clear and instructive overview, and then look at the detailed worked examples in Chapter 8.

Metaphors We Live By by G Lakoff & M Johnson, Univ. of Chicago (1980). A stimulating and very readable discussion of the way that metaphor permeates language, affecting how we think and use language.

Index